CAPTIVATED

Also by Thabiti Anyabwile

CAPTIVATED

**Beholding the Mystery of
Jesus' Death and Resurrection**

Thabiti M. Anyabwile

Reformation Heritage Books
Grand Rapids, Michigan

Reformation Heritage Books
2965 Leonard St. NE
Grand Rapids, MI 49525
616-977-0889 / Fax 616-285-3246
orders@heritagebooks.org
www.heritagebooks.org

Printed in the United States of America
14 15 16 17 18 19/10 9 8 7 6 5 4 3 2 1

Library of Congress Cataloging-in-Publication Data

Anyabwile, Thabiti M., 1970-
  Captivated : beholding the mystery of Jesus' death and resurrection / Thabiti M. Anyabwile.
      pages cm
  ISBN 978-1-60178-300-4 (pbk. : alk. paper) 1. Jesus Christ—Crucifixion. 2. Jesus Christ—Resurrection. I. Title.
  BT450.A59 2014
  232.96'3—dc23
                          2013042553

For additional Reformed literature, request a free book list from Reformation Heritage Books at the above regular or e-mail address.

To Afiya,

our firstborn daughter,
born to survive.
You bring us such joy.
May you thrive in your knowledge of Jesus
and find your highest happiness in Him.

Contents

Acknowledgments

I've never done anything worthwhile except it was a surprising work wrought by God's gracious hand. Preaching and writing are not exceptions. I'm surprised I have the sacred privilege of declaring the oracles of God and sometimes see the water of my sermons turned into wine for His people. I owe all honor, praise, adoration, and thanks to God above all, who by His grace makes more of our lives and labors than we could ask or think.

I also want to extend a special thank-you to my daughter, Afiya. As part of a work experience program at her high school, she joined the staff of First Baptist Church as my editor on this project. Her presence, insight, and keen mind for writing were a great blessing to this father who delights in his children. She is a gifted writer even at an early age, and I pray she puts her gift for editing and writing to great use for the Savior. Thank you, Sweetie, for all you give to your dad.

My wife of more than two decades deserves hazard pay. She has been beside me and sometimes before me every step of the way. She is far, far better than I deserve. I know no greater source of earthly encouragement or loving accountability. I see you in my eyes, and I thank you for being my wife and partner in life.

The saints of First Baptist Church of Grand Cayman have for seven years now listened to my preaching with interest and patience. You've made me a better preacher, and you didn't have much to work with. Thank you for coming every Sunday, for putting the Word to work in your lives, for seeking Jesus and for loving one another. It is a great privilege to serve you.

To the entire team at Reformation Heritage Books: Thank you for the opportunity to work together on this project. Special debt is owed to Jay Collier, who proposed turning these sermons into a book. Without his prompting, it is unlikely this book would ever have seen print.

Introduction

Parents teach their young children not to stare. "It's not polite," we say. "Don't point." Eventually we socialize our children into the habit of making eye contact—but not for too long. We teach them not to gaze upon others and to feel awkward or suspicious if other people stare at them. We make ourselves and our children expert glancers, visual skimmers, ocular snapshot takers.

I wonder if this cultural habit affects our ability to peer into matters that deserve a long look. How, for instance, does our aversion to staring at others affect our ability to behold the face of the Lord? Might we be conditioned to steal quick peeks at Jesus without tracing with the eyes of faith the thorn-induced scars on His brow, the lash-transferred welts on His back, or the nail-inflicted piercings in His hands and feet?

How would our knowledge of Jesus, our friendship with Him, and our familiarity with His ways be deepened if we looked long at Him? If we learned to stare, gaze, behold—look at Him and what He has done?

I believe the Bible implores and commands us to take a long look at Jesus. From Isaiah's "Behold your God!"

(40:9), to the psalmist's "taste and see that the Lord is good" (34:8), to Jesus' own invitation to "take My yoke" (Matt. 11:29), the Scriptures find diverse ways to beckon the faithful to a luxuriant look at the Son of God.

Perhaps the Scriptures most forcefully beckon us to "come and see" when various writers ask profound questions in connection with Jesus' crucifixion and resurrection. Those questions drive us to consider not just the events themselves but also their meaning. The Scriptures question us so that we might look beneath the surface to find more of the never-ending treasures of Christ.

When Jesus asks that the cup of God's wrath be passed from Him, what does it mean when the Father remains silent? How should we understand the Lord's cry from the cross, "My God, My God, why have You forsaken Me?" When the apostle Paul asks rhetorically, "O Death, where is your sting? O Hades, where is your victory?" (1 Cor. 15:55), and the angel asks the women at the tomb, "Why do you seek the living among the dead?" (Luke 24:5), what are we meant to know about the defeat of death and the Christian hope? What might we know about knowledge itself, our epistemology, when we consider the two travelers to Emmaus asking the resurrected Lord, "Do you not know these things?" (Luke 24:18).

Genuine contemplation of these questions requires we set aside our early lessons about politeness for a while and stare into the mystery of the cross and resurrection. What follows is an attempt to do just that—to stare at Jesus and be captivated by Him. I pray these meditations, originally a series of Easter sermons I preached at First

Baptist Church of Grand Cayman, help lock our eyes on Jesus. As we are transfixed, may we find that He has been looking upon us all along. May we behold His face and be satisfied as we're changed from one degree of glory to another in Him.

Chapter 1

Is There No Other Way?

Jesus prayed, "O My Father, if this cup cannot pass away from Me unless I drink it, Your will be done."
—MATTHEW 26:42

"Is there no other way?" It's the kind of question we ask when life reaches its most difficult points: when a long, slow illness steals the strength and vitality of a loved one; when a deeply troubled marriage stands on the cliff of divorce; when a desperate search for work, food, and shelter results only in hunger and homelessness or crime and begging; when an addiction becomes a fast track to rock bottom and despair; when depression closes in and makes the whole world dark…again. In these times, the question sneaks into our minds and sometimes escapes our lips: "Is there no other way?" Have you ever asked God that question?

When the brokenness of this world and our lives reaches its most intense, most threatening moments, we are tempted to think we are the only ones who have asked that question or felt that sorrow. But would it surprise you to know that you are not alone? Even God the Son in His incarnate life on earth at His point of greatest agony asked that question: "Is there no other way?"

The truth of Jesus' crucifixion and resurrection is a daily reality for those who believe in Him. Yet from time to time, that daily reality requires extended contemplation and reflection, and we should ponder its meaning so that it does not become daily neglected. Christians need deeper glimpses into the mystery of God and His salvation. We need times of slow, contemplative consideration of the wonder of Christ's work for us. To do so, we begin with a question inspired by events in the garden of Gethsemane as they are recorded in Matthew 26. We begin by pondering a question hurting people have asked throughout the ages: "Is there no other way?"

As we ponder this question, we find that God's one perfect will accomplishes far more than all our imagined alternatives. A no from God does more for our good than a yes to all our dreams.

A New Experience for the Son of God

In Matthew 26, Jesus faces impending betrayal. He retreats to a somewhat secluded garden called Gethsemane. This is one of the rare occasions in the entire New Testament when we learn something of Jesus' mental state. In verse 37, Matthew tells us Jesus "began to be sorrowful and deeply distressed."

Being "sorrowful and deeply distressed" was a new experience for Jesus. Jewish religious leaders had tried to capture and kill Him on several previous occasions, but He seemed undaunted. The "time had not yet come," so the Lord passed through those attempts on His life like ships sailing through mists. But Gethsemane is different.

God the Son, the Son of God, feels sorrowful and very heavy. Jesus says in verse 38, "My soul is exceedingly sorrowful, even to death."

Those words probably shook and shocked Peter, James, and John. The disciples had never heard the Master speak this way about death—about anything. In fact, Jesus had taught them that He came in order to be killed for sins and to rise again. He had even rebuked Peter for protesting against that teaching. But that was when His time had not yet come. Now the time *has* come, and Jesus faces the hour of betrayal and death. The Lord tells us He could die from the overwhelming sorrow He feels.

Have you ever been so sorrowful and troubled that you thought the sorrow itself might kill you? Have you ever been so grieved of soul you thought you could curl into a fetal position and pass away?

Jesus is so troubled that He reaches out to His friends for support: "Stay here and watch with Me" (v. 38). His sleepy friends make His sorrow worse when they fail His small request to watch and pray (vv. 40, 43). They didn't pray *with* Him, nor did they pray *for* Him. They slept right up to the moment of His betrayal (v. 45). Our Lord had to awaken His friends so they wouldn't sleep through His betrayal. Have you ever been troubled, and your friends let you down in your hour of need?

During this nighttime solitary vigil, Jesus asks the Father three times, "Is there any way other than what's ahead?"

> He went a little farther and fell on his face, and prayed, saying, "O My Father, if it is possible, let this cup pass from Me."…

> Again, a second time, He went away and prayed, saying, "O my Father, if this cup may not pass away from me unless I drink it, Your will be done."...
>
> So he left them, went away again, and prayed the third time, saying the same words. (vv. 39, 42, 44)

At Jesus' baptism, the voice from heaven said, "This is My beloved Son, in whom I am well pleased" (Matt. 3:17). At our Lord's transfiguration, Heaven spoke and said again, "This is my beloved Son, in whom I am well pleased. Hear Him!" (Matt. 17:5). Heaven had always answered prayers from the Son of God. But in Gethsemane, there is only the stony silence of the cold desert night. Heaven closes its mouth and refuses to speak aloud. Jesus asks, "Is there any other way?" In the silence comes an answer: "No, this is the only way." To look more deeply into this mystery, we must ask, "*Why* is this the only way?" For the following reasons, the Father's no and the cross are absolutely necessary.

We Need a High Priest Who Can Identify with Us

Jesus must be able to identify with our weaknesses in order to represent us before God. The Lord faces the most significant and troubling moment of His earthly life and endures the sorrow He feels because He must enter into our weakness.

Hebrews 4:15 tells us why Jesus shares our humanity: "For we do not have a High Priest who cannot sympathize with our weaknesses, but was in all points tempted like as we are, yet without sin." This sharing in our weakness was absolutely necessary. Hebrews 2:17 teaches, "Therefore, in all things He had to be made like His brethren, that He might be a merciful and faithful High Priest in things pertaining to God." Our Lord had to embrace our flesh in order to represent us to God.

Sometimes when we suffer, we can tell if our comforters have ever really endured what we are experiencing. We can tell by their words—they tend to talk too much or to share clichés. We can tell by their attitudes—they tend to be impatient with our grief. We can tell by their actions—they tend to move too quickly to the next thing and forget us in our suffering.

We do not need a high priest like our human comforters—unmoved, impatient, forgetful. We need a High Priest who can sympathize with our weaknesses. We need a representative before God the Father who will be merciful and faithful to us.

We must not miss the Bible's crucial teaching at this point. In order for us to have the sympathizing, merciful, and faithful High Priest who knows what our lives are like and who never leaves us nor forsakes us, the Son of God *had* to be made like us and endure our sorrow. He *had* to take on our humanity, share in our temptation, and taste our suffering. This is why when Jesus prays, "Can you remove this cup?" and "Is there another way?" the Father answers with a loving, tender, and silent, "No—this is the only way for You to become their perfect High Priest."

Now that Jesus has become such a High Priest for Christians, Hebrews 4:16 encourages us: "Let us therefore come boldly unto the throne of grace, that we may obtain mercy and find grace to help in time of need." The trouble and sorrow of Gethsemane and Calvary open the grace and help of the throne.

To Reveal That the Father Is Compassionate

If we want to know God the Father and understand His character, we must study Jesus. As we see Jesus in agony in Gethsemane, we must not forget we are also seeing the Father's character.

In Matthew 11:27 Jesus says, "All things have been delivered to Me by My Father, and no one knows the Son except the Father. Nor does anyone know the Father except the Son, *and the one to whom the Son wills to reveal Him*" (emphasis added). Do you see? We cannot know the Father unless the Son reveals Him to us. And Jesus' entire life—whether He is in miraculous power or garden brokenness—reveals the Father. The Son is "the brightness of [the Father's] glory and the express image of His person" (Heb. 1:3).

So what are we witnessing when we see Jesus facedown on the ground, sorrowful and troubled, asking the Father if He must drink the cup of God's judgment? When we watch Jesus, we see the moving and dynamic unveiling of the Father's heart. Jesus reveals to us a heavenly Father who is not far off from us or unconcerned about our needs and suffering. The Father is not remote and unmoved. The Father is sorrowful and troubled too. Weeping and sorrowful, Jesus dramatically reveals to us what is meant in 2 Corinthians 1:3 when God is called "the Father of mercies and God of all comfort."

The One who cries out in the garden is not just the incarnate Son of God. Through the Son, the Father shows us His mercy and love. Through the Son, the Father says, "I know what it's like," and He enters our suffering and takes it as His own. Because the Son suffered, we have both a sympathetic High Priest *and* an understanding and sympathetic heavenly Father. The no that Jesus receives is the yes to our salvation. The silent no reveals the Father's love for us.

Sometimes in our suffering and trials, we fall into the trap of thinking, "Jesus knows all of my sorrows, but the Father"—and we mistakenly think "the real God"—"doesn't care very much." Have you ever thought or felt this way? If we think that way, we eventually begin to feel even farther away from God and Jesus. Have you ever noticed that?

The simple reason is this: If Jesus reveals the Father, and we think the Father is far off, then we will eventually feel Jesus is far off since Jesus and the Father are one. What we learn about Jesus gives us a window into the character of the Father. Jesus is touched with sorrow and trouble. Thus, He reveals a Father sorrowful over sin and brokenness. Jesus calls to the Father for what is best. The answer reveals a Father who gives only the best for His children—even if the answer is no and costs the life of His one and only Son.

There simply was no other way than the cross to reveal the truth that inspired these lyrics:

> How deep the Father's love for us,
> How vast beyond all measure
> That He should give His only Son
> To make a wretch His treasure

> How great the pain of searing loss,
> The Father turns His face away
> As wounds which mar the chosen One,
> Bring many sons to glory

At Gethsemane, we see the Father's compassionate heart in a prostrate Son. Along with His compassion, God is holy, so there is yet another reason Heaven answers no to Jesus' question.

Jesus Is the Only Possible Mediator between God and Man

We think of gardens as serene, peaceful places. We visit them to quietly enjoy beauty and reflection. However, in Gethsemane that night, bombs dropped and exploded. A spiritual war took place—a war between a holy God who hates sin and an unholy humanity that hates God. God and sinful man have been hostile toward one another since sin entered the world in Genesis 3. It's that way today. For even today, "the carnal mind is enmity against God; for it is not subject to the law of God, nor indeed can be" (Rom. 8:7). The Bible wraps all the hostility between God and man in this question: "Is there another way?" Can anything other than the cross of Jesus Christ end the war between Omnipotence and depravity? Is there anyone who can step in and reconcile the two? Is there a mediator who can bring peace?

The answer comes to us from 1 Timothy 2:5–6: "For there is one God and one Mediator between God and men, the Man Christ Jesus, who gave Himself a ransom for all, to be testified in due time." Or, as the apostles put it in Acts 4:12: "Nor is there salvation in any other, for there is no other name under heaven given among men whereby we must be saved."

People often imagine they "can make peace with God." People near death are often asked, "Have you made your peace with the Maker?" But peace with God cannot be negotiated. Our offense and war has been so long and protracted that we can't simply say "uncle" and expect that His wrath or our hearts will be changed. We need someone to broker a truce—someone the Father trusts, someone who can represent God's interests and our interests perfectly.

Only Jesus ends the war between God and man with a peaceful solution. If Jesus does not go to the cross, then God will win the war with a final and terrible judgment against man for his sin. Sinners cannot fight God and win. Having Jesus as our Mediator is the only way for us to be reconciled to God.

Only Jesus Could Make Atonement for Our Sin

The cup Jesus must drink is the cup of God's wrath. God's wrath is His totally righteous and pure anger and resolved action against evil and sin. It is His moral purity provoked by moral evil. The wrath of God is being revealed against all the ungodliness of men (Rom. 1:18).

In Gethsemane, Jesus faces *all* God's wrath against *all* the evil and sin committed by *all* His people throughout *all* time.

Imagine, if you can, *all* the anger of God over *all* the sins ever committed by *all* His people who have ever lived concentrated and poured *all* at once into a cup to drink. Is it any wonder the Savior confesses to being sorrowful and troubled even unto death?

But it must be this way. Consider again Hebrews 2:17. First, the writer explains that Jesus had to be made like us in every way in order to be our High Priest. But he gives a second reason the Lord had to be made like us and drink the cup: "to make propitiation for the sins of the people." Humanity owes God a sacrifice. This "propitiation for sins," or atonement, is the sacrifice that turns away the wrath of God. It is the kind of sacrifice that puts two divided parties "at one" again. Humanity owes this atonement, but we cannot supply it because of our sin and imperfection.

Good works will not atone for sin. "All our righteousnesses are like filthy rags" (Isa. 64:6) before our holy God. Animal sacrifices will not do. "For it is not possible that the blood of bulls and goats could take away sins" (Heb. 10:4). Religious practices will not atone. Such regulations "are of no value against the indulgence of the flesh" (Col. 2:23).

Only a sinless, perfect offering could ever atone for the sins of the world. Unless Jesus, the perfect, spotless Lamb of God, drinks the cup of God's wrath, every person will have to drink God's judgment himself. Unless Jesus drinks the cup, every person will forever be separated from the love of God. There will be no escape and no reconciliation.

Jesus *must* drink the cup of God's wrath—and He did. He drank all of it. So sinners may now rejoice with the truth of 1 John 4:10: "In this is love, not that we loved God, but that He loved us and sent His Son to be the propitiation for our sins." Do you feel ashamed that your sin put the Son of God face down in the dirt, pleading for another way? Do you feel ashamed that your sin is so vile and wretched that there was no other way?

The Father said to the Son, "No, it must be this way," so that His wrath would be propitiated—satisfied and turned away from sinners. The cross was the *only* way to atone for our sins. But the cross is not just about our needs. There is more to the cross even than that. The cross is mainly about God and His agenda.

To Prove the Father's Righteousness

Did you know that until Gethsemane, Calvary, and the empty tomb, God's righteousness was in question? Romans 3:24–26 tells us that "God set forth [Christ Jesus] as a propitiation by His blood, through faith, to demonstrate His righteousness, because in His forbearance God had passed over the sins that were previously committed, to demonstrate at the present time His righteousness, that He might be just and the justifier of the one who has faith in Jesus."

Why did God present Jesus Christ as a "propitiation," or sacrifice of atonement? Was it only to save sinners? It was to save sinners, but it was also to achieve something more. God presented Jesus as an atoning sacrifice "to demonstrate His righteousness," or prove His justice.

But why was that necessary? It was necessary "because in His forbearance God had passed over the sins that were previously committed." All the sins before Jesus' death on the cross had not yet been punished. God had passed them over. But at the same time God had accepted some sinners as His own people. How could He accept some unpunished sinners as His own and reject other unpunished sinners at the same time? How could God do that and still be considered righteous? That was the problem created by God's salvation prior to the cross of Calvary.

And this was one reason the Father said no in Gethsemane. A cosmic contradiction needed to be put right. So God presented Jesus Christ as an atoning sacrifice "to demonstrate His righteousness, because in His forbearance God had passed over the sins that were previously committed, to demonstrate at the present time His righteousness, *that He might be just and the justifier of the one who has faith in Jesus*" (emphasis added). For all the centuries up until Jesus' incarnation and crucifixion, the Father had passed over the sins of His people. The people had offered up symbolic sacrifices, but those did not really atone for sin. They were shadows, not the reality.

Since the time of Adam's sin and Israel's redemption, a question had hung over God's head. The universe wondered how God could be righteous. When Jesus prayed in Matthew 26:42, "If this cup cannot pass away from Me unless I drink it," the Father's justice, or righteousness, was at stake. If Jesus does not drink the cup and atone for sins, God will be proven to be unfair. As John Piper puts it, "This is the most significant problem in the universe." Is God unfair?

The one silent no in Gethsemane resounds in double duty in answer to the centuries-long question of whether God was fair to forgive. The cross proves that God is just in punishing sinners and in forgiving sinners who trust in

Jesus Christ. The cross was absolutely necessary in order to vindicate the righteousness of God. Without the cross, God remains open to the charge of unfairness and injustice. Jesus' death as an atoning sacrifice paid the debt of all those who believed in God's promise of a coming salvation before Jesus' incarnation. By the same sacrifice, those who had faith before Christ's advent and those who have faith since find righteousness with God and righteousness in God. When Jesus asks if there is another way, the Father says, "No, because My righteousness must be upheld."

The Father and the Son's Glory Must Be Revealed

God's greatest motivation for all His actions is the revelation of His glory in the universe. Everything He does is to show to the creation His own perfect beauty and flawless attributes. This is supremely true with our Lord's cross. When Jesus asks if there is any other possible way, it is as if He is asking, "Is there another way to reveal Your glory more perfectly?" The answer cloaked in silence is no. The cross is the greatest possible revelation of the glory of God the Father and God the Son.

Consider the apostle John's account of Jesus' betrayal in chapter 13. Immediately after Judas left the Last Supper to betray Jesus, the Lord says to the disciples, "Now the Son of Man is glorified, and God is glorified in Him. If God is glorified in Him, God will also glorify Him in Himself, and glorify Him immediately" (vv. 31–32). When Jesus announces that the hour has come, He not only means His betrayal is about to happen but also that *through* that betrayal, His crucifixion and resurrection, the hour for the mutual glorification of Father and Son has arrived. So Jesus prays in John 17, "Father, the hour has come. Glorify Your Son, that Your Son also may glorify You.... I have glorified You on the earth. I have finished the work which You have given Me to do. And now, O Father, glorify Me together with Yourself, with the glory which I had with You before the world was" (vv. 1, 4–5).

The Father and Son agree to the crucifixion and resurrection as the ultimate means for each to bring the other the highest possible glory in the universe. Heaven remained silent in response to Jesus' prayer in order to see this glory manifested. No more perfect way existed for the beauty, splendor, weightiness, and fame of God—Father, Son, and Holy Spirit—to be displayed except Jesus drink the cup of God's wrath and accomplish our salvation.

Conclusion

This cry for another way has tremendous consequences for us. The only way for us to please and glorify God is by picking up our cross daily and following Jesus. In Gethsemane, Jesus shows us not only what God has done for man but also what man owes to God.

Man owes God complete submission to His will. In Gethsemane, the only perfect Man bowed before God and concluded His prayer, "Nevertheless, not as I will, but as You will" (Matt. 26:39). Such is the heart mankind should have before God—a heart of complete submission and faith.

Do you desire God's perfect will for your life? Do you wonder what God's perfect will is? Jesus says in John 6:40, "And this is the will of Him who sent Me, that everyone who sees the Son and believes in Him may have everlasting life; and I will raise him up at the last day."

God's will for us includes two steps. First, we must look to Jesus. Perhaps we have looked everywhere else. If we have looked closely, we have discovered that there is no other way to God. We must now turn from all other hopes and ideas and turn to Jesus.

Second, believe in Jesus. Receive Him and trust Him as He offers Himself in the gospel. He offers Himself to you as your God—crucified, buried, and resurrected—to glorify the Father and save you from God's wrath. Believe He is your only Mediator with God, your perfect High Priest who knows your weaknesses and brings you to God as a friend and servant, not an enemy.

This is God's will for us—look to Jesus Christ and believe in Him alone for salvation. God wills to give eternal life and the promise of the resurrection to all who look to and believe on His Son. Let us not harden our hearts. Let us submit to the Spirit's call to Christ in the gospel— perhaps for the first time. Confess your sin. Turn away from sin. Let us put our hope in Jesus to deliver us, to make us new, and teach us to live by God's will. Turn to Jesus from your sin and trust Him to give you eternal life and to be your sacrifice that turns God's wrath away.

Those who understand why the silent no was so necessary have abundant reason to rejoice. We should not think an answer was not given on that amazing night in Gethsemane. Nor are we to think that the Father's silent no indicated neglect, as though God the Father were a "divine deadbeat dad." Rather, we are to understand that the only perfect Father found occasion to deny the only perfect Son because such denial achieved the only perfect goals: a perfectly qualified high priesthood, reconciliation through the only God-man Mediator, loving atonement for the sins of men, the vindication of the Father's righteousness, and the ever-redounding glory of the Father in the Son and the Son in the Father. Gethsemane's silent answer rings eternally in the loud joyous praises of the universe.

Because the Father answered no, sinners have a merciful and faithful High Priest perfectly intimate with all their weaknesses. We have One we can approach for grace. Because the Father answered no, we have One who stands between us in all our ungodliness and God in all His holiness to reconcile us and reunite us as friends rather than rebels. Because the Father answered no, those who have faith in Christ need never fear the Father's wrath again; His anger has been fully satisfied in the Son's atonement. Because the Father said no, we stand assured that our acceptance with God happened on completely legitimate grounds—no parlor tricks, no loopholes, no legal fiction, no injustice to threaten or question the exchange of our sin for Jesus' righteousness. Because the Father said no, we will forever enjoy and share the glory of Father and Son in the unending, timeless age to come.

I am so glad the Father said no.

For Further Gazing and Reflection

1. Read Matthew 26:36–45. Describe Jesus' circumstances in this passage. Explain why He would ask, "Is there no other way?"

2. The Father said no to the Son for several reasons. What is the Bible's teaching in Hebrews 2:14–18 and 4:14–16 about why the Father said no?

3. In His garden brokenness, what does Jesus reveal to us about the Father?

4. What parties were at war in the garden of Gethsemane? Who brought an end to the war, and how did He accomplish it?

5. Why couldn't we drink the cup of God's wrath for ourselves? Why could only Jesus drink it, and what did His drinking it accomplish?

6. What was the "cosmic contradiction" that needed to be set right? How did God set it right?

7. What is the ultimate reason the Father said no?

Chapter 2

Why Have You Forsaken Me?

Jesus cried out, "My God, My God, why have You forsaken Me?"
—MATTHEW 27:46

"Leave no man behind" is part of the creed that armed services men and women swear to one another and their country. This commitment drives ordinary men and women to extreme lengths in loyalty to their fellow soldiers. In southern Afghanistan, British Royal Marines went to extreme lengths to rescue one of their own, displaying their heroism on January 15, 2007. After two hundred marines assaulted a Taliban stronghold, they discovered that, upon leaving the area, one of their men had been left behind. Since there might still be Taliban in the area, the marines needed to act speedily to rescue their fellow soldier. So they utilized the only helicopters available, three AH-64 gunships, to carry marines back to the area. Since AH-64s have room inside for only a two-man crew, the other marines harnessed themselves on the helicopters' two stubby wings, usually used to carry rockets and missiles. The three helicopters quickly reached the scene of the battle. The four marines dismounted from the wings of the helicopters and found their fellow soldier, who had been killed in battle. They tied his body to the wing of the third helicopter, and all three gunships returned to their base. That is taking "leave no man behind" seriously.

Many of us have seen the moving picture of five U.S. soldiers planting the American flag atop Mount Suribachi in Iwo Jima. Perhaps few of us know that the soldier who took the picture was killed in battle nine days later, and his body was not recovered. In 2007, sixty-two years after Sergeant William H. Genaust was killed, an effort was made to retrieve his body. *Sixty-two years later!* Why a search after such a long time? Their effort was driven by the commitment to "leave no man behind"—not even his remains.

Such a commitment represents loyalty to the highest degree, just as intentionally leaving a man behind represents betrayal to the highest degree. Soldiers cannot justify forsaking their comrades in battle. We call that cowardice. Such a man is a "Benedict Arnold" to his comrades. Such abandonment cannot be redeemed, nor does it redeem others.

We all have had experiences with being let down, disappointed, and even abandoned. Most of our betrayals have been minor: the way friends casually make promises they fail to keep or the way coworkers and employers play politics in the office. Occasionally people experience much harsher abandonments—stabbings in the back—such as a spouse breaking a marriage vow or a parent abandoning them. In those situations we have been left behind in the worst of ways. We can barely cope in such times.

And so we look in wonder at the greatest abandonment ever to occur, when God the Father abandoned God the Son on Calvary's cross. When we consider the separation of Father and Son at Calvary, we stare into the deep mystery and meaning of the cross and the resurrection. But the Father's abandonment of Jesus leads to the sinner's adoption. God abandons one perfect Son in order to adopt millions of sinful sons. It is the only abandonment with any honor and redemption.

A Day of Judgment

In the last chapter, we saw our Savior facedown in agony in Gethsemane, pleading in prayer, "Is there any way other than drinking this cup?" We received the silent answer from heaven: "No, there is no other way." Jesus had to drink the cup.

In this chapter we come to the Passover celebration in Jerusalem. The crowds of Jewish faithful make the pilgrimage to the Holy City with songs and rejoicing. The entire city is festive—except one nearby place.

We leave the singing crowds of Jerusalem and go to Golgotha (v. 33), the place of the skull. We find Jesus on a hill called Calvary outside Jerusalem—drinking the cup He could not avoid, the cup the Father would not take away from Him. It seems all the people were there when they crucified our Lord: soldiers (v. 36), thieves (v. 38), blaspheming crowds (v. 39), and religious leaders (v. 41). And God was there when they crucified our Lord.

We know God was there because darkness smothered daytime: "Now from the sixth hour until the ninth hour there was darkness over all the land" (v. 45). The sixth hour refers to noon. From noon to three in the afternoon, when the sun normally blasts at full strength, *darkness came over all the land*. Luke 23:45 simply states that the sun stopped shining. This was no eclipse. At Passover the moon is full. It is impossible to have an eclipse when the moon is full. Besides, when is the last time you heard of an eclipse lasting three full hours? There is nothing natural about this scene. This is *super*natural. God was there.

The darkness represents judgment. Do you remember the first Passover in Exodus 10, when God tells Moses to stretch out his hand toward heaven "that there may be darkness over the land of Egypt, darkness which may even be felt" (vv. 21–23)? With the ninth plague, darkness covered the whole land before God killed Egypt's firstborn.

Egypt lay in darkness for three days, Jerusalem for three hours. After the darkness, Egypt's firstborn sons were killed; in Jerusalem the only begotten Son of God was slain. In Egypt, a lamb's blood covered the doorposts of homes. In Jerusalem, the Lamb of God's blood covered the sins of the world.

The darkness of Calvary means judgment has come on Israel. Prophets declared that this day of judgment would come. The prophet Amos told of a day when Israel's judgment would be ripened and God would spare them no longer.

> "And it shall come to pass in that day," says
>   the Lord GOD,
> "*That I will make the sun go down at noon,*
> *And I will darken the earth in broad daylight;*

I will turn your feasts into mourning,
And all your songs into lamentation;
I will bring sackcloth on every waist,
And baldness on every head;
I will make it like mourning for an only son,
And its end like a bitter day." (Amos 8:9–10,
    emphasis added)

God judged the entire land in supernatural darkness. But God judged Jesus too. We know this because of His cry from the cross. Notice that Jesus "cried out with a loud voice" (v. 45). This was no peaceful sleep in a quiet darkness. Jesus does not ease into death with a cherubic face wrapped in soft, glowing light. He screams. Some pains are too great to be suppressed.

The Lord suffers a singular, incomparable agony. The word used for "loud voice" occurs only here in the entire New Testament. Here, alone, at the cross, the Lord cries out to God and does not call Him "Father." Jesus speaks in Aramaic rather than Hebrew, Greek, or Latin—as if some cries cannot be pronounced in a foreign tongue. There are traumas so deep only your mother tongue will do.

But what amazes us is this loud, emotional, and mysterious cry—"My God, My God, why have You forsaken Me?" We are captivated on this dark noonday by that word *forsaken*. What can it mean to be forsaken by the Father? One theologian calls this "one of the most impenetrable mysteries of the entire Gospel narratives." Angels desire to look into it. Yet God records this mystery for us to consider. How could the Father abandon the Son? We learn at least three things about the nature of the

Father's abandonment of Jesus when we stare deeply into this mystery.

The Father Allowed Jesus to Suffer Social Abandonment

We see that Jesus was socially abandoned when we consider the responses of the people who were at Golgotha that day. First, the soldiers scoff and mock. See how they ridicule the Savior:

> Then the soldiers of the governor took Jesus into the Praetorium and gathered the whole garrison around Him. And they stripped Him and put a scarlet robe on Him. When they had twisted a crown of thorns, they put it on His head, and a reed in His right hand. And they bowed the knee before Him and mocked Him, saying, "Hail, King of the Jews!" Then they spat on Him, and took the reed and struck Him on the head. And when they had mocked Him, they took the robe off Him, put His own clothes on Him, and led Him away to be crucified....
>
> Then they crucified Him, and divided His garments, casting lots, that it might be fulfilled which was spoken by the prophet:
>
> "They divided My garments among them,
> And for My clothing they cast lots."
>
> Sitting down, they kept watch over Him there. And they put up over His head the accusation written against Him:
>
> THIS IS JESUS THE KING OF THE JEWS. (vv. 27–31, 35–37)

The anonymous faces in the crowd passed by, mocking and reviling a man they did not know. They blasphemed, wagged their heads, and said, "You who destroy the temple and build it in three days, save Yourself! If You are the Son of God, come down from the cross" (vv. 39–40).

The religious leaders scorned Him too. These were the teachers of Israel and the stewards of God's Word—the ones who should have known best of all. But instead, the Lord faced "the chief priests...mocking with the scribes and elders" (v. 41). They mocked Him as Savior: "He saved others; Himself He cannot save." They mocked Him as King: "If He is the King of Israel, let Him now come down from the cross, and we will believe Him" (v. 42). They mocked His faith: "He trusted in God; let Him deliver Him now if He will have Him" (v. 43). They mocked Him as Son, saying with sarcasm: "He said, 'I am the Son of God'" (v. 43). They mocked everything about our Lord.[1]

Even thieves persecuted the Savior and "reviled Him with the same thing" (v. 44). We see them all: the soldiers, the religious leaders, the thieves, and the crowd. All of them rejected and mocked Jesus.

But we cannot see how complete His social alienation was until we ask, "Where were His disciples and friends?" Our Lord's friends all scattered and abandoned Him too. Only a few women stood and watched from some distance far away (vv. 55–56). To be forsaken meant to be socially outcast and cut off from every strata of society.

---

1. Charles H. Spurgeon, *Commentary on Matthew: The Gospel of the Kingdom* (Edinburgh: Banner of Truth, 2010), 428.

At the broadest level, Jesus suffered abandonment by being forsaken by those He came to save. We must ask ourselves this: "If I was there at Golgotha, would I have responded to the stripped and beaten Galilean the same way?"

The Father Allowed Jesus to Suffer Emotional Desertion

Can you sense the emotional torture in the Savior's cry? *"My God, My God, why have You forsaken me?"* Who can read those words, imagine that scene, and not shudder in horror? In that anguished cry, we get a sense of the emotional desertion Jesus felt when God forsook His Son. Jesus' cry is a quotation of David in Psalm 22:1. As a messianic psalm, Psalm 22 clearly points far beyond David's experience to Jesus the Messiah. The psalm is best read when we understand it comes from Jesus' lips.

In the first half of Psalm 22 we see four contrasts that give us a glimpse of the emotional intensity of Jesus' cry. These contrasts are really gaps between Jesus' expectation and God's actions on that day. Forsakenness is not simply a matter of loneliness; it includes loneliness and something deeper. Neither is forsakenness simply a matter of being let down. Forsakenness blends loneliness and being let down with what feels like an element of emotional betrayal—at least the betrayal of unfulfilled expectations.

We saw at the beginning of the chapter that troops in the armed services pride themselves on never leaving a man behind on the battlefield. To leave troops and fellow soldiers stranded represents the greatest betrayal. That is forsakenness. Or imagine the groom dressed in his tuxedo awaiting his bride. He expects to see her dressed in white, slowly gliding down the aisle, but he unexpectedly learns that she has left him at the altar. That is forsakenness. An expectation, a longing, a hope…knifed in the back. Forsakenness is to be cast off, abandoned, deserted, left, spurned, ditched, marooned, walked out on, jilted. Forsakenness carries all the emotional thrust of a knife in the back or a punch in the gut.

Consider the four contrasts in Psalm 22 as an illustration of the emotional forsakenness Jesus felt on the cross. We may experience these things in our human trials, but Christ Jesus, perfect man and perfect God, experienced these things to a degree we cannot imagine.

First, we experience feelings of emotional desertion if our prayers go unanswered by the sovereign God we trust. Consider the words of Psalm 22:2–3:

> O My God, I cry in the daytime, but You do not hear;
> And in the night season, and am not silent.
> But You are holy,
> Enthroned in the praises of Israel.

God rules all things. He sits enthroned and is high and lifted up. Yet this sovereign God does not answer the incessant cries and prayers of the One who trusts in Him. We have the sense that the righteous prayers of righteous men ought to be answered by a righteous God. If God does not grant such a man his prayers, he feels a gap, a sense of forsakenness. The more righteous the man and the prayer, the more forsaken he feels. There was never a man more righteous than Jesus. Never did a person experience a deeper sense of forsakenness from unanswered prayers than Jesus felt on Calvary's cross. In the cry of dereliction, we hear the Son of God pleading, "My God, My God, how could You not answer My cry when You rule all things?"

Second, we experience feelings of emotional desertion when the righteous are forsaken and sinners are delivered. When we see God deliver others while He allows us to be mocked and persecuted, our sense of emotional abandonment is heightened. In Psalm 22:4–5, Jesus calls to mind God's deliverance of Israel:

> Our fathers trusted in You;
> They trusted, and You delivered them.
> They cried to You, and were delivered;
> They trusted in You, and were not ashamed.

David points out that God delivered Israel—sinful, backsliding, stiff-necked Israel that repeatedly turned from God to idols. In the past, God had delivered them and rewarded their trust. But verses 6–8 contrast the treatment backsliding Israel received with the treatment Jesus received.

> But I am a worm, and no man;
> A reproach of men, and despised by the people.
> All those who see Me ridicule Me;
> They shoot out the lip, they shake the head, saying,
> "He trusted in the LORD, let Him rescue Him;
> Let Him deliver Him, since He delights in Him!"

Psalm 22 was written hundreds of years before Jesus was born, but it forecasts Matthew 27 verbatim. How could God deliver a sinful people such as Israel and leave the perfect Son of God to suffer the mockery of men He created? For that matter, how could God deliver a sinful people such as us and leave the perfect Son of God to suffer abandonment? The gap intensifies Jesus' emotional desertion. We might imagine the cry of dereliction to include, "My God, My God, how could You abandon Me to insults when You have delivered backsliders?"

Third, when faithfulness is repaid with abandonment, then feelings of emotional desertion increase. That was David's experience, expressed in Psalm 22:9–11.

> But You are He who took Me out of the womb;
> You made Me trust while on My mother's breasts.
> I was cast upon You from birth.
> From My mother's womb
> You have been My God.
> Be not far from Me,
> For trouble is near;
> For there is none to help.

How might we feel if we had trusted and obeyed God for years, only to be left alone and without help in our time of need? The sense of emotional betrayal increases.

Jesus was miraculously conceived by the virgin Mary. He lived to do the Father's will. The only trouble the Lord gave His earthly parents was when He was twelve years old and remained too long in the temple teaching the religious leaders. From birth Jesus served the Father. But now, in trouble on the cross, the Lord cries with a loud voice, "My God, My God, why have You forsaken Me?" Yet no help came from heaven. Feeling abandoned after He had lived a life of perfect obedience and trust left the

Son of God overwhelmed with emotion. We might hear in the cry of dereliction, "My God, My God, how could You leave Me alone after I did all You asked?"

Fourth, our feelings of desertion rise when our enemies are close but our God seems far off. We see this in Psalm 22:12–21. Notice the prophecies pointing to our Lord:

> Many bulls have surrounded Me;
> Strong bulls of Bashan have encircled Me.
> They gape at Me with their mouths,
> Like a raging and roaring lion.
>
> I am poured out like water,
> And all My bones are out of joint;
> My heart is like wax;
> It has melted within Me.
> My strength is dried up like a potsherd,
> And My tongue clings to My jaws;
> You have brought Me to the dust of death.
>
> For dogs have surrounded Me;
> The congregation of the wicked has enclosed Me.
> They pierced My hands and My feet;
> I can count all My bones.
> They look and stare at Me.
> They divide My garments among them,
> And for My clothing they cast lots.
>
> But You, O Lord, do not be far from Me;
> O My Strength, hasten to help Me!
> Deliver Me from the sword,
> My precious life from the power of the dog.
> Save Me from the lion's mouth
> And from the horns of the wild oxen!
>
> You have answered Me.

Bulls, lions, dogs, and wild oxen surrounded the Lord on that day. These were men turned to beasts by their sin and blindness. The Savior feels His heart melting, His bones dislodged, and His strength dried up. His hands and feet are pierced, and He is stripped naked and leered at while His clothes are divided. Here is the creator of the world hanging seemingly powerless, looking to the Father to be His strength. But the Father stands far off—farther away than the women who were there. Yahweh, who was His strength, withdrew. Jesus' heart melted and failed. Can you imagine a greater sense of abandonment than being left by God? In the cry of dereliction we hear the Son crying, "My God, My God, where are You when I'm scared and weak?"

Psalm 22 helps us understand what is happening emotionally to our Lord in those final moments on the cross. Not only was the Savior socially abandoned by the people He came to save, but He was also emotionally deserted by the Father in whom He trusted. But there is at least one more aspect to Jesus' abandonment.

The Father Allowed Jesus to Suffer Spiritual Separation

This is the deepest, darkest part of Jesus' suffering. Social abandonment was horrible, but it came from outside. Emotional desertion was painful, but it was limited to Jesus' internal frame of mind. This spiritual forsakenness, this spiritual separation from the Father, occurs deep within the Godhead itself. We dare not speculate

lest we blaspheme. But Jesus must have felt like something was torn in the very fabric of His fellowship with
the Father.

To get a sense of this, we must remember what the
relationship between Father and Son had been from eternity past. The opening words of the apostle John's Gospel
tell us, "In the beginning was the Word, and the Word
was with God, and the Word was God. He was in the
beginning with God" (vv. 1–2). For all eternity, Jesus lived
with the Father. And not just *with* the Father. The Greek
word *pros,* translated "with," can have the sense of "to" or
"toward." Jesus Christ, the eternal Word, lived with the
Father, turned toward Him in face-to-face fellowship. All
the Lord Jesus had ever known was the loving, approving,
shining face of His Father.

To be turned face-to-face with God the Father is the
Bible's idea of the highest possible blessing and happiness.
This is why God teaches Moses to bless the Israelites in
Numbers 6:24–26 with the words:

> The LORD bless you and keep you;
> *The LORD make His face shine upon you,*
> And be gracious to you;
> *The LORD lift up His countenance upon you,*
> And give you peace. (emphasis added)

Having the Lord's face shining upon them became the
highest aspiration and hope among the holy and righteous. So 1 Chronicles 16:10–11 exhorts the faithful:

> Glory in His holy name;
> Let the hearts of those rejoice who seek the LORD!

> Seek the LORD and His strength;
> *Seek His face evermore.* (emphasis added)

The Psalms repeatedly include that last exhortation—
"Seek His face always!" That is man's highest and happiest
ambition.

But conversely, having the Lord turn His face *away* results
in the deepest fear and dread. So David brings together that
high and holy aspiration to seek God's face with that deep
and fearful dread when he writes in Psalm 27:8–9:

> When You said, "*Seek My face,*"
> My heart said to You, "*Your face, LORD, I will seek.*"
> *Do not hide Your face from Me*;
> Do not turn Your servant away in anger:
> You have been my help;
> *Do not leave me nor forsake me,*
> O God of my salvation. (emphasis added)

Our incarnate Lord could easily have spoken the words of
Psalm 27 at Golgotha. For in His earthly life and ministry, the Lord Jesus continually sought the Father's face. He
sought to live in a way that earned the Father's approval
and favor. And He did.

But on that dark midday on Golgotha, when the sun
refused to shine, the unimaginable and indescribable happened. That beautiful, shining, loving face of the Father
withdrew into the dark, frowning, punishing face of
wrath. He who knew no sin was made to be sin for us
(2 Cor. 5:21). The Son of God Himself "bore our sins in
His own body on the tree" (1 Peter 2:24). He became
accursed for us, "for it is written, 'Cursed is everyone who

hangs on a tree'" (Gal. 3:13). And when our sins were laid upon Him, Jesus felt the full, horrible truth of Habbakuk 1:13—that God the Father is "of purer eyes than to behold evil, and cannot look on wickedness." At three o'clock that dark Friday afternoon, the Father turned His face away, and the ancient, eternal fellowship between Father and Son was broken. In the terror and agony of it all, Jesus cried, *My God, My God, why have You forsaken Me?*"

The deepest, most dreadful thing had happened. In his commentary on Matthew 27:46, John Calvin describes it: "This was his chief conflict, and harder than all the other tortures.... For not only did he offer his body as the price of our reconciliation with God, but in his soul also he endured the punishments due to us.... Nothing is more dreadful than to feel that God, whose wrath is worse than all deaths, is the Judge.... He maintained a struggle with the sorrows of death, as if an offended God had thrown him into a whirlpool of afflictions."

In Jerusalem that day hung a picture of hell as the Son of God was cut off socially from everyone, was deserted emotionally on the cross, and was separated spiritually from the eternal Father with whom He had always lived face-to-face. That is hell. That was our deserved place! That horror awaits all those who die in their sin. In the face of such judgment, even the God-man cried out and died.

We must remember and treasure that Jesus willingly suffered all this so sinners can escape it. Jesus' abandonment means the sinner's adoption. He took our place on the cross so we can take His place in the kingdom. Because He was abandoned socially, we become children in the household of God. Because He was deserted emotionally, we become whole again—renewed in the image of God. Because He suffered spiritual separation, we are now spiritually united to Him through faith, never to be separated from God's love. Because He was forsaken, we are forgiven. It is finished! Our salvation has been completed. We need only to turn from sin and trust in Jesus.

It is not just veterans of war who return to reclaim their fellow soldiers' bodies. When they return to a battlefield, they look for dead and buried soldiers. But three days after His Son was buried, the Father reclaimed a resurrected and living Lord! Jesus was not finally forsaken, and neither is anyone who trusts in Him. If we need evidence to sustain our trust, remember this: the Father went back for the body. He raised Jesus from the grave, and now He lives and rules in glory.

For Further Gazing and Reflection

1. Read Matthew 27:27–46, which describes the "greatest abandonment ever to occur." Who was being abandoned—and by whom? Why was this the only abandonment with any honor and redemption?

2. How do we know that judgment occurred at Calvary? Who was being judged?

3. What different individuals and groups contributed to Jesus' social abandonment while He was on the cross?

4. Read Psalm 22:1–21. From this passage, describe the emotional desertion the Son experienced on the cross.

5. What was the deepest part of Jesus' suffering on the cross? Why was it the source of His greatest suffering?

6. How do we know that Jesus ultimately was not abandoned?

Chapter 3

Where, O Death, Is Your Victory?

"O Death, where is your sting? O Hades, where is your victory?"
—1 CORINTHIANS 15:50–58

Each gospel writer tells us that Jesus died on the cross:

> And Jesus cried out again with a loud voice, and yielded up His spirit. (Matt. 27:50)

> And Jesus cried out with a loud voice, and breathed His last. (Mark 15:37)

> And when Jesus had cried out with a loud voice, He said, "Father, 'into Your hands I commend my spirit.'" Having said this, He breathed His last. (Luke 23:46)

> So when Jesus had received the sour wine, He said, "It is finished!" And bowing His head, He gave up His spirit. (John 19:30)

Jesus died. The fact is so commonplace it seems unnecessary even to mention it. Almost hollow. Almost as if we've said nothing new or meaningful. But *new* and *meaningful* are often two different things.

Many of us have become accustomed to thinking that meaning comes from newness. Old truths are still true and therefore still meaningful. But just because a truth is familiar, because we have heard it before, does not mean we can pass it by without reflecting on its meaning. Jesus *died. Jesus* died. What can it mean to say the Son of God died? And how should the Christian respond to that news?

As we stare into the ineffable realities of the cross and the resurrection, we discover another tremendous inheritance for the Christian. We discover that, as the Puritan John Owen put it, the death of Jesus Christ means the death of death itself. Moreover, the death of death in the death of Jesus Christ also means victory over death for those who trust in Christ as their God and Savior.

Death is dead. We have won.

The Death of Jesus Christ Means the Death of Death

Can you imagine how the obituaries in Jerusalem might have read some two thousand years ago? If there had been such a thing as a *Jerusalem Herald,* Friday's readers might have noticed the account of three crucifixions of two thieves and a person the paper described as an "upstart messiah" who had been sentenced for blasphemy. Another infamous rebel, Barabbas, had apparently escaped execution when the throngs of people shouted for his release and called for the condemnation of Jesus in the rebel's place. Officials were unavailable for comment given the holy celebrations scheduled for the weekend.

But Tuesday's paper would have featured a strange obituary indeed. An old enemy of every living person was put to death. Perhaps the brief article would have the headline "Death Is Dead." For, three days following His crucifixion, our Lord rose victorious over death and the grave.

What Death Is

We want to linger in the three days during which the Author of life lay buried in a cave. We really want to consider the nature of death—and Jesus' death specifically. In order to understand what it means to say Jesus died, we need to consider what death means.

A Curse

The Bible tells us that death is a curse. Do not think of witch doctors and voodoo when you hear the word *curse.* Who was the first one to mention dying in the Bible? It was God at the beginning of creation, who cursed mankind with death when sin entered the world through Adam and Eve.

Do you remember the scene in the garden of Eden? "The Lord God planted a garden eastward in Eden, and there He put the man whom He had formed. And out of the ground the Lord God made every tree grow that is pleasant to the sight and good for food. The tree of life was also in the midst of the garden, and the tree of the knowledge of good and evil" (Gen. 2:8–9). Everything, as God said at the end of each day of creation, was good.

Then, we read in verses 15–17, "the Lord God took the man and put him in the garden of Eden to tend and keep it. And the Lord God commanded the man, saying, 'Of every tree of the garden you may freely eat; but of the tree of the knowledge of good and evil you shall not eat, for in the day that you eat of it you shall surely die.'" Verse 17 records the first mention of death in all of creation. I wonder if Adam understood what *death* meant and how horrible it would be. No one had ever died. Man was not made to die. He was made to live with God in obedience and love forever.

But when Adam and Eve disobeyed God and sin entered the world, God kept His promise to curse mankind with death in Genesis 3:17–19:

> Then to Adam He said, "Because you have heeded the voice of your wife, and have eaten from the tree of which I commanded you, saying, 'You shall not eat of it':
>
> "Cursed is the ground for your sake;
> In toil you shall eat of it
> All the days of your life.
> Both thorns and thistles it shall bring forth
>   for you,
> And you shall eat the herb of the field.
> In the sweat of your face you shall eat bread
> *Till you return to the ground,*
> For out of it you were taken;
> *For dust you are,*
> *And to dust you shall return.*" (emphasis added)

God cursed the ground and curses sinful man to return to the ground. God pronounced a life-ending sentence against sinful mankind. Death is a curse.

A Wage

The Bible describes death as a wage. Through Adam sin entered the world, and through sin death came. Romans 6:23 says, "The wages of sin is death." Death is the salary sinners take home, but it doesn't pay well. Sin rewards with slaughter. It kills. Because we are all infected with the disease of sin and commit sin, we all die.

An Enemy

The Bible calls death an enemy. Jeremiah 9:21 paints a poetic picture of death as a stalking, stealing enemy:

> For death has come through our windows,
> Has entered our palaces,
> To kill off the children—no longer to be outside!
> And the young men—no longer on the streets!

Death stalks and threatens us like a vengeful enemy, and this is why we hate it so. We deserve death because of our sin, but we hate it because of life. Death claims us all. That is why 1 Corinthians 15:26 tells us, "The last enemy that will be destroyed is death."

Agony

Death is agony. In Luke 16, the Lord Jesus Christ tells a parable about a rich man and a poor beggar named Lazarus. The rich man lived luxuriously and dined sumptuously. The poor man, Lazarus, lived off the crumbs from the rich man's table. Their lives could not have been more different. Then they both died. The rich man went to Hades, or hell. Lazarus, the poor man, went to

Abraham's bosom, or heaven. Luke 16:23–24 describes the rich man's agony:

> And being in torments in Hades, he lifted up his eyes and saw Abraham afar off, and Lazarus in his bosom. Then he cried and said, "Father Abraham, have mercy on me, and send Lazarus that he may dip the tip of his finger in water and cool my tongue; for I am tormented in this flame."

Notice a couple of things in this account: First, hell does not cure the rich man of his sinful pride and privilege. He still expects Lazarus to serve him in hell. Second, hell reverses the two men's fortunes. The first shall be last and the last shall be first. Now, in death, the rich man looks for drops of water just as Lazarus hunted crumbs of bread in life.

Death is not a peaceful sleep or a long nothing. It is not lights out—and that's it. Death is torment. It includes a conscious experience of anguish and pain.

Both Physical and Spiritual

We can speak of both a physical and a spiritual death. An unsaved person faces the prospect of both a bodily death and a spiritual death. We hardly have to turn to the Bible to prove that people die physically. We have evidence all around us, don't we? Our personal experience with death in our families and among our friends should prove to us that the Bible is true, that the curse is real. There has been a steady march of death since the moment Adam and Eve sinned. Genesis 5 records the steady, stomping cadence of death. Repeatedly we read "and he died"—eight times (vv. 5, 8, 11, 14, 17, 20, 27, 31).

"*And he died.*" The extraordinarily long lives that men lived, recorded in the early chapters of Genesis, amaze us. But no matter how long they lived, the one constantly recurring truth is they died. That sentence describes nearly everyone ever born. Sin and death is the one biblical doctrine for which we have perfect empirical evidence. The death rate is one-to-one. The words of Ecclesiastes 7:2 present profound wisdom: "For [the day of death] is the end of all men; and the living will take it to heart." Are you taking to heart the certainty of death, our enemy, God's curse—not just physical death but spiritual also? Are you taking to heart spiritual death?

Spiritual death means to be cut off from God. A person may be alive and strong physically but dead as a doorknob spiritually. In the past, when prisoners on death row approached execution, guards or other prisoners customarily announced, "Dead man walking. Dead man walking." That proclamation was a way of acknowledging that though the prisoner was yet alive, he was as good as dead.

The Bible tells us that the world is full of spiritually dead men walking: "And you He made alive, who were dead in trespasses and sins, in which you once walked according to the course of this world, according to the prince of the power of the air, the spirit who now works in the sons of disobedience." Moreover, "we were dead in trespasses" (Eph. 2:1–2, 5). This is the spiritual death that leaves sinful people unable and unwilling to do anything that pleases God, cuts them off from Him, and makes them hostile toward Him. This is the reality for every person who is not born again and united to Jesus Christ by faith. Such a person is a spiritually dead man walking, awaiting his or her final execution.

Occurs Twice for Unbelievers

Death occurs twice for unbelievers. If a person dies in his sins, impenitent, unforgiven by God through Jesus Christ, then he also experiences the "second death" at the end of time when God judges all mankind. Hebrews 9:27 proclaims, "It is appointed for men to die once, but after this the judgment." The Bible calls the judgment that follows the physical death of unbelievers "the second death" in Revelation 20:

> Then I saw a great white throne and Him who sat on it, from whose face the earth and the heaven fled away. And there was found no place for them. And I saw the dead, small and great, standing before God, and books were opened. And another book was opened, which is the Book of Life. And the dead were judged according to their works, by the things which were written in the books. The sea gave up the dead who were in it, and Death and Hades delivered up the dead who were in them. And they were judged, each one according to his works. Then Death and Hades were cast into the lake of fire. This is the second death. And anyone not found written in the Book of Life was cast into the lake of fire. (vv. 11–15)

Revelation 21:8 lists those who experience the second death: "the cowardly, unbelieving, abominable, murderers, sexually immoral, sorcerers, idolaters, and all liars shall have their part in the lake which burns with fire and brimstone, which is the second death." How sadly mistaken are all those who think that we need to face only this life and only one physical death. How tragic! A life and death exist beyond what we experience on this earth. The second death fixes a person permanently in a state of separation from God, in which he experiences conscious torment and receives the curse and wages of sin.

We understand why people fear death and why that fear holds them in chains. Who wants God's cursing judgment? Who looks forward to God repaying him for his sins? Who welcomes defeat at the hands of a ruthless enemy? Who longs to experience unending agony? Who likes to think of a second, spiritual, unending death?

Yet this is what awaits all those who die apart from faith in Jesus Christ. God has prepared a place of wrath, death, and conscious torment for those who do not obey the gospel of our Lord. So we fear death. We instinctively kick against it and try to push it back. No one apart from the seriously ill or those without their proper senses welcomes death. Death is an unwelcome visitor.

Are you afraid of death? If you are not afraid of your own, are you afraid about someone else's? If you are not a Christian and you are thinking correctly, probably you are afraid. Curse, repayment, agony—death is a fearsome enemy. But there is good news.

Jesus' Death Means Victory over Death
for Those Who Believe

So why does Paul rejoice so boldly in the face of death in 1 Corinthians 15:55? He writes, "O Death, where is your sting? O Hades, where is your victory?" If death is as horrible and effective an enemy as I've been describing, why does Paul boast in death's face? Has Paul gone mad? Certainly not—Paul boasts in the face of death for several reasons.

Jesus Destroyed Death

In his second letter to Timothy, the apostle Paul reminds his young friend that the saving grace of God has appeared through "our Savior Jesus Christ, *who has abolished death and brought life and immortality to light through the gospel*" (2 Tim. 1:10, emphasis added). Death is dead. Jesus destroyed it in His death and resurrection. It was impossible that death should ever have victory over the Author of life. God raised Jesus up, "having loosed the pains of death, because *it was not possible that He should be held by it*" (Acts 2:24, emphasis added).

Though we see people still dying, a time fast approaches when the experience of death will be done away with. That is what Paul means in 1 Corinthians 15:54 when he writes, "So when this corruptible has put on incorruption, and this mortal has put on immortality, then shall be brought to pass the saying that is written: 'Death is swallowed up in victory.'" Or, as John the beloved disciple puts it in Revelation 20:14: "Then Death and Hades were cast into the lake of fire." In other words, death and Hades, or the grave, die the second death too. In the age to come, Jesus destroys the existence of death and death as an event for those who believe. This is why Paul rejoices.

Jesus Destroyed the One Who Had the Power of Death
Jesus not only destroyed death but also the power behind death. Jesus did not simply get rid of the symptom; He eliminated the cause too: "Inasmuch then as the children have partaken of flesh and blood, He Himself likewise shared in the same, that *through death* He might *destroy him who had the power of death, that is, the devil*" (Heb. 2:14, emphasis added).

Jesus' death not only destroys death, but it also destroys the one who came to kill, steal, and destroy. Satan reigned through death and terror, but Jesus Christ conquered Satan's kingdom and ended his reign through His own death. So the resurrected Lord triumphantly proclaims, "I am He who lives, and was dead, and behold, I am alive forevermore. Amen. And I have the keys of Hades and of Death" (Rev. 1:18). Because Jesus conquered the power *of* death and the power *behind* death, Paul rejoices. The keys of death and hell are in the hands of his ever-living Redeemer!

Jesus Freed Believers from the Fear of Death
and the Mastery of Sin
Hebrews 2:14–15 tells us how Jesus' death frees us from our fear of death: "Inasmuch then as the children have partaken of flesh and blood, He Himself likewise shared in the same, that through death He might destroy him who had the power of death, that is, the devil, and release

those who through fear of death were all their lifetime
subject to bondage." Romans 6:5–10 explains how Jesus'
death frees us from the mastery of sin:

> For if we have been united together in the like-
> ness of His death, certainly we also shall be in
> the likeness of His resurrection, knowing this,
> that *our old man was crucified with Him,* that
> the body of sin might be done away with, that we
> should no longer be *slaves of sin. For he who has
> died has been freed from sin.* Now if we died with
> Christ, we believe that we shall also live with
> Him, knowing that Christ, having been raised
> from the dead, dies no more. Death no longer has
> dominion over Him. For the death that He died,
> He died to sin once for all; but the life that He
> lives, He lives to God. (emphasis added)

Death and sin no longer master the Christian. The
Christian lives free from the law of sin and death through
the death and resurrection of Jesus Christ. Paul rejoices in
the face of death because death can no longer control him.

Death Cannot Separate Us from the Love of God
Near the end of Romans 8, Paul writes that in Christ, we
will always know God's love. He gives a long list of things
that cannot separate the Christian from the Father's love
in Christ Jesus. Do you remember how Paul begins the
list? He writes, "For I am persuaded that neither death
nor life…shall be able to separate us from the love of God
which is in Christ Jesus our Lord" (Rom. 8:38–39).

Because Jesus put death to death, we are assured that nothing—not even death—can tear us away from the Father's love. In fact, Psalm 116:15 tells us, "Precious in the sight of the LORD is the death of His saints." God now takes pleasure in the death of His saints because death simply transfers the believer into the full communion of His love. So Paul rejoices and mocks death.

An Old Truth with a Fresh Meaning Revisited

Jesus died. Death is destroyed. Satan, the one who holds the power of death, is destroyed. Death and sin no longer have mastery. Death cannot separate us from the love of God. This is why the gospel, when it is properly understood, floods a person with such delight and boldness in the face of death. This is why Paul seems to sing: "O Death, where is your sting? O Hades, where is your victory?"

Paul explains that "the sting of death is sin, and the strength of sin is the law" (1 Cor. 15:56). The word Paul uses for "sting" calls to mind a wasp's stinger or a snake's fangs. The stinger or fang releases the venom that causes pain or death.

Death was accustomed to winning the victory in every human case. But in His death and resurrection, the Lord Jesus Christ ripped the fangs from Satan's mouth. He plucked the stinger from the wasp of death. The Lord Jesus perfectly obeyed the law and then became sin for us. That is why Paul rejoices, "Thanks be to God, who gives us the victory through our Lord Jesus Christ" (1 Cor. 15:57).

The death of death in the death of Christ means victory for those who believe in Him. Jesus destroyed death and brought life and immortality to light through the gospel. Eternal life and immortality come to all those who believe that Jesus died and rose again to save sinners. This is the most basic promise of the gospel. We hear this promise over and over again throughout the New Testament. It is an old truth with fresh meaning. Christian, read these promises and stand in them. If you are not yet a believer in Jesus Christ, read these promises and pray for grace to receive them by faith today.

If you place your trust in Jesus Christ alone as your God and rescuer, you will never taste death:

> Most assuredly, I say to you, he who hears My word and believes in Him who sent Me has everlasting life, and shall not come into judgment, but has passed from death into life. (John 5:24)

> Most assuredly, I say to you, if anyone keeps My word he shall never see death. (John 8:51)

> Jesus said to her, "I am the resurrection and the life. He who believes in Me, though he may die, he shall live." (John 11:25)

If you truly repent of sin and follow the Lord in faith, you will be justified and reconciled through Jesus' death:

> [Jesus] was delivered up because of our offenses, and was raised because of our justification. (Rom. 4:25)

> We were reconciled to God by the death of His Son. (Rom. 5:10)

> Or do you not know that as many of us as were baptized into Christ Jesus were baptized into His death? Therefore we were buried with Him through

baptism into death, that just as Christ was raised from the dead by the glory of the Father, even so we also should walk in newness of life.

For if we have been united together in the likeness of His death, certainly we also shall be in the likeness of His resurrection. (Rom. 6:3–5)

If you trust in Jesus Christ alone for salvation, the curse of death will be removed through His death:

Christ has redeemed us from the curse of the law, having become a curse for us (for it is written, "Cursed is everyone who hangs on a tree.") (Gal. 3:13)

All those who follow Jesus in saving faith will be free from the second death:

He who overcomes shall not be hurt by the second death. (Rev. 2:11)

Blessed and holy is he who has part in the first resurrection. Over such the second death has no power, but they shall be priests of God and of Christ, and shall reign with Him a thousand years. (Rev. 20:6)

If you are not yet a Christian, believe on Jesus Christ. Believe His Word, which promises victory over death and eternal life. Believe He was crucified—and, by grace, that He died in your place to suffer your agony and curse. Believe that three days later He rose again victorious over death and Satan. Believe that He is coming again to take His people into heaven with Him. Believe He and the Father love you, and nothing shall separate you from their love. Believe on Jesus, and you will be saved from sin and death, Satan, and suffering to live a new life of righteousness and hope through faith in the Son of God. Repent from sin and believe, and you will be saved.

Christian, the death of Jesus means your victory over death. Stand firm in this victory. Let nothing move you or scare you. When you think of yourself or your loved ones and death comes to mind, sing with Paul, "O Death, where is your sting? O Hades, where is your victory?" Rejoice, for your last enemy has been defeated. Through faith in the resurrected Lord, you will live forever in His love.

Death is dead. Believers have won. Believe on Jesus.

For Further Gazing and Reflection

1. Read 1 Corinthians 15:50–58. Why does the apostle Paul say in this passage that God gives us victory over death when we all will still die, just as Jesus died?

2. What does Genesis 3:17–19 teach us about death?

3. What are the two types of death? Describe what each one means.

4. What is the second death described in Revelation 20:11–15? Who will experience it?

5. What good news do 2 Timothy 1:10, Hebrews 2:14–15, and Romans 8:38–39 give us about death?

6. Read John 11:25. How can it be that we may die, yet live?

Chapter 4

Why Do You Seek the Living among the Dead?

The angels said, "Why do you seek the living among the dead?"
—LUKE 24:5

Luke 24 opens with the women walking to the Lord's tomb very early in the morning. These women have names and stories. Verse 10 tells us Mary Magdalene walked with them. The Lord cast seven demons out of this Mary. What was she thinking and feeling as she walked? What was she remembering?

Joanna went with them to the tomb. Joanna regularly traveled with Jesus (Luke 8:3). She helped support Jesus' travels and preaching financially. Her husband worked as a manager in King Herod's household. Did this woman of means, who was perhaps accustomed to getting things accomplished, feel powerless now?

Then there was Mary, the mother of James, an apostle Jesus chose. She too journeyed to the tomb. Did she think of James's friendship with Jesus, of the void there would be in her son's life?

As you can see, these were women with names and stories. They traveled "very early in the morning" (v. 1), literally at "deep dawn," or twilight—when the sky mixes purple from night and orange from morning, making up its mind whether to go on sleeping or shine in glory. Do you think the women walked slowly or quickly? Did they chat a lot or step in soft silence? Did the walk feel long or short, as if each step covered a centimeter or a mile?

I imagine their walk was too purposeful to be a slow trudging. But perhaps they were too exhausted to walk briskly. Remember the events of the last three days. Just three days earlier, Jesus was betrayed and sentenced to death. The betrayal broke His disciples' hearts in two ways. First, their long-awaited Messiah was dead. Second, one of their trusted leaders, one of the Twelve, sold Jesus out for thirty pieces of silver. The entire nation seemed to turn against them overnight—the religious leaders, the Roman government, the people. The movement they believed in seemed to be over. And that was not the worst part.

They were there. They experienced the midday darkness (Luke 23:44–45). They heard that terrible cry: "*My God, My God, why have You forsaken Me?*" And they watched Him breathe His last breath (Matt. 27:46, 50). They could have written the lyrics for that famous hymn: the disciples were there when they crucified our Lord.

They knew Joseph of Arimathea requested the body and prepared a tomb. "The women who had come with Him from Galilee followed after, and they observed the tomb and how His body was laid." They were there. Jesus was buried on the day before the Sabbath—Preparation Day. On Preparation Day, "they returned and prepared spices and fragrant oils" to bury Jesus properly (Luke

23:55–56). *But how can you be prepared to bury the Son of God?*

Luke 23:56 says, "They rested on the Sabbath according to the commandment." I am quite sure they obeyed the law and stopped their activities. It likely seemed the thing to do: return to the law, its familiar customs, its granite requirements. So they endeavored to rest. But have you ever tried to rest after a loved one's death?

Their minds probably replayed the scenes all day long: the lashing, the soldiers' mocking, the jeering crowds, the blood. So much blood! Their hearts grieved over and over again. With nothing to distract them, they probably found no real rest for their souls. And there were still things to do to bury the Lord properly.

So, on the third day—the first day of the week, Sunday—they rose very early in the morning and walked to the tomb, with hearts nearly too heavy to carry. Sorrow filled their steps. Mourning was on their minds. They took "certain other women with them" and "the spices which they had prepared" and went to the tomb (v. 1). They expected to complete their mourning rituals even if they had not completed their mourning.

But often in the Bible, dawn, or early morning, is the time God uses to make new revelations. Sunrise is when the Lord often surprises His people. That Sunday morning, God surprised the women with three amazing things.

Three Surprises

First, "they found the stone rolled away from the tomb" (v. 2). Matthew 27:60 tells us Joseph of Arimathea "rolled

a large stone against the door of the tomb, and departed."
Mary Magdalene and Mary the mother of James sat oppo-
site the tomb watching Joseph as he sealed the grave with
the stone (27:61). Mark 16:3 tells us that on the way to the
tomb, "they said among themselves, 'Who will roll away
the stone from the door of the tomb for us?'" The women
expected a difficult barrier. But, to their surprise, "when
they looked up, they saw that the stone had been rolled
away—for it was very large" (16:4).

Second, "they went in and did not find the body of the
Lord Jesus" (v. 3). Nothing was where it was supposed to
be. They found the stone moved and the body missing.
Imagine the rush of confusion and fear. You witness the
Lord being crucified, and you see Him die. You watch
Joseph bury His body and seal the tomb. You are certain
Jesus is dead. But now the grave is empty.

Imagine the fear and anger. Who took the body? Who
would be so godless as to do it on the Sabbath during the
holiest religious festival of all? Why?

John 20:1–2 tells us Mary Magdalene took off running
as soon as she saw the stone was rolled away. She ran to
Peter and John, saying, "They have taken away the Lord
out of the tomb, and we do not know where they have laid
Him." She was thinking of grave robbers—not the grave
robbed. The rest of the women stood in the tomb "per-
plexed" (v. 4). Mark tells us the women "trembled and were
amazed" and were "afraid" (16:8). The body was gone!

Third, "two men stood by them in shining garments"
(v. 4). A misplaced stone surprised them. A missing
body startled them. Now messengers shock them. Mark

describes "a young man clothed in a long white robe sitting on the right side" (16:5). Matthew says an angel had come from heaven, rolled back the stone, and sat on it. John does not mention the angels but instead focuses on the folded grave clothes. Luke tells us in verse 23 that the two men were, in fact, angels.

Angels beaming and glorious frightened the women. The ladies bowed their faces to the ground, not just to hide them from the frightening bright light. Simply turning away would do that. They bowed in reverence and awe of such majestic beings.

The women had no idea they would meet heaven's angels at an early morning graveside. But what these angels said next was perhaps the greatest surprise. It was a question: "Why do you seek the living among the dead?" (v. 5).

The Question

I do not know which is more surprising: that the angels asked a question rather than made a bold announcement, or the actual question the angels asked. Angels are messengers of God. Since their message comes from God, we might think that all their sentences end in exclamation marks. But here, they ask an incisive question. Perhaps there is a message in the fact that the angels asked a question just as there is a message in the question they asked: "Why do you seek the living among the dead?" The question produces a Copernican revolution in the way we view all of life and existence. It reorients and redirects everything.

Redirects Us from Death to Life

Clearly the women visited the tomb to see a dead man. We do not stop by a graveside to entertain living people. These women had seen Jesus die and be buried. Their minds were on death. But the death of Jesus means the death of death itself. The angels' question clearly indicates they will not find Jesus among the dead. They must not think of the Lord as dead.

Christian recording artist Shai Linne captures the contrast between Jesus and every other world religious leader on precisely this issue. He writes:

> Plato is dead, Socrates is dead
> Aristotle and Immanuel Kant are dead
> Neitzsche and Darwin are dead—however
> Jesus is alive
>
> Buddha is dead, Mohammed is dead
> Ghandi and Haile Selassie are dead
> Elijah Mohammed is dead—however
> Jesus is alive

All life lived apart from the resurrection is really a slow death. We must find Christ where there is life. So many people simply live to die, and some are dying to live. But the resurrection means you can live to live. Christians do not visit tombs and shrines to meet with God. We visit the Alpha and the Omega, the Resurrection and the Life, to find life itself. This question—if we listen and receive it—reorients us from death to life. It calls us to seek the living Savior and the life He gives.

Redirects Us from the Cross to the Resurrection

We Christians rightly love the cross. The cross symbol-
izes and proves God's love for sinful humanity. We make
our boast in the cross. But this question—"Why do you
seek the living among the dead?"—exposes something
often true of us. Like these Sunday morning mourners,
we sometimes forget that something magnificent exists
beyond the cross and gives it its glory. If we get stuck on
the cross without contemplating the resurrection, then our
faith feels like death rather than life. Our faith remains
stuck on tragedy without triumph. The resurrection adds
triumph to the tragedy!

This question reminds us that Jesus rose from the grave.
God raised Him up. When we embrace the meaning and
import of this question, we find ourselves reoriented—no
longer bound by the decades of life we have on earth but
expecting the resurrection life that will never end. These
women look for Jesus among the resurrected living, and
we too look for Jesus in the resurrection that is to come.
We live this life like people who will be raised to life again.

Do you live with death or the resurrection in view?
Do you actively live as though God raised the dead? What
would such living look like?

Life lived in light of the resurrection includes radical
sacrifices in faith. Hebrews 11:17–19 illustrates this truth.
It tells us how Abraham's belief in the resurrection prepared him to make the most radical sacrifice for God:
"By faith Abraham, when he was tested, *offered up Isaac,*
and he who had received the promises offered up his only
begotten son, of whom it was said, 'In Isaac your seed

shall be called,' *concluding that God was able to raise him up*, even from the dead, from which he also received him in a figurative sense" (emphasis added).

Life lived in light of the resurrection looks like a life of sacrificial love. We discover this in the gospel of John. Jesus teaches in John 10:11: "I am the good shepherd. The good shepherd gives His life for the sheep." In John 10:17–18 the Master tells us how the resurrection enables Him to give His life: "Therefore My Father loves me, because I lay down My life that I may take it again. No one takes it from Me, but I lay it down of Myself. I have power to lay it down, and I have power to take it again. This commandment I have received from My Father." John considers Jesus' example of radical love and teaches us that every Christian should love this way: "By this we know love, because He laid down His life for us. And we also ought to lay down our lives for the brethren" (1 John 3:16). And why not love this way? Our lives will be raised again together with our risen Lord.

Life lived in light of the resurrection realizes that knowing Jesus and being with Jesus is the greatest possible future. We learn that from the apostle Paul in Philippians 3:10–11. Paul's goal was to "know Him and the power of His resurrection, and the fellowship of His sufferings, being made conformed to His death, if, by any means, I may attain to the resurrection from the dead.

"Why do you seek the living among the dead?" moves us from the death of the cross to the life of the resurrection. That redirection enables us to live lives of radical sacrifice, love, and hope.

Redirects Us from Emotions to Scripture

Imagine the range of emotions these women and the other disciples experienced during those three days: mourning, confusion, fright (vv. 4–5). With all their swirling emotions, they must have been tempted to interpret all that happened through their feelings. We can feel so deeply that we give our feelings the last word. We can say, "I don't care what they say or what the facts are or even what the Bible says. I know how I feel!"

But this question—"Why do you seek the living among the dead?"—confronts the authority of their emotions by pointing to a higher authority, a surer source of knowing. The question points to God's Word. Specifically, it points to Jesus' teaching in Galilee in verses 6 and 7: "Remember how He spoke to you when He was still in Galilee, saying, "The Son of Man must be delivered into the hands of sinful men, and be crucified, and the third day rise again."

Notice that key word *remember.* Never underestimate how remembering God's Word will change and steady your emotions when the most tragic and surprising things happen in life. The disciples' emotions should not have been rooted in their experiences but in Jesus' teaching. They should have been oriented to God's promises found in His Word. The Lord Himself had tried to prepare them by turning them from their emotions to His promise. Remember how He did that in John 14:1–4:

> Let not your heart be troubled; you believe in God, believe also in Me. In My Father's house are many mansions; if it were not so, I would have told you. I go to prepare a place for you. And if I

go and prepare a place for you, I will come again
and receive you to Myself; that where I am, there
you may be also. And where I go you know, and
the way you know.

We most need redirection from emotion to Scripture
when our feelings are strongest and our experiences surprising. In such situations we need to be turned to God's
Word because this is when our feeble hearts and minds
are most vulnerable. This question powerfully redirects
the mourning disciples from their emotions and fear to
the solid promises and reality of the gospel. Living in light
of the resurrection keeps us living in light of God's promises. Do you actively live in that light?

Redirects Us from Current Events to God's Providence
These women—and all the disciples—were shaken by the
events of the previous three days. The same was true of
the disciples on the road to Emmaus in Luke 24:13–18:

Now behold, two of them were traveling that
same day to a village called Emmaus, which was
seven miles from Jerusalem. And they talked
together of all these things which had happened.
So it was, while they conversed and reasoned, that
Jesus Himself drew near and went with them. But
their eyes were restrained, so that they did not
know Him.

And He said to them, "What kind of conversation is this that you have with one another as you
walk and are sad?"

Then the one whose name was Cleopas answered and said to Him, "Are You the only stranger

in Jerusalem, and have You not known the things
which happened there in these days?"

These disciples were focused on the things that had
happened in recent days. Ironically, current events had
them trapped—locked in the past and unaware of the
future. But these Emmaus disciples were not very *current*
at all. They pondered the actions of men but were in dan-
ger of missing the actions of God.

We can be like that too. All we see is what has happened lately. We start to sound like an eighties pop song,
asking God, "What have You done for me lately?" But then
God's question comes back to us: "Why do you seek the
living among the dead?" The question reorients us from
current events to God's providence.

When the angels explain what they mean by their
question, one little word tips us off, helping us recognize
the importance of God's sovereign providence. Do you see
that word "must" in Luke 24:7? "The Son of Man *must* be
delivered into the hands of sinful men, and be crucified,
and the third day rise again" (emphasis added). The verbs
"be delivered," and "be crucified" are passive. Men are
doing these things to Jesus; He is not doing these things to
Himself. But that word "must" tells us Someone else also
acts in, through, behind, and above sinful men. Providence is at work. The invisible hand of God brings about
things that *must* happen according to His plan, including
the third verb in that sentence—Jesus *must* rise again. The
resurrection, above all other events, reminds us to look for
God's providence in history.

We see this most clearly in Acts 2:22–24. On the day of Pentecost, the apostle Peter stands to preach the first recorded Christian sermon. And this is what Peter proclaims:

> Men of Israel, hear these words: Jesus of Nazareth, a Man attested by God to you by miracles, wonders, and signs which God did through Him in your midst, as you yourselves also know—Him, *being delivered by the determined purpose and foreknowledge of God*, you have taken by lawless hands, have crucified, and put to death; whom God raised up, having loosed the pains of death, because it was not possible that He should be held by it.

"Being delivered by the determined purpose and foreknowledge of God" is a fancy theological way of saying "must." The angels' question and explanation are designed to help the disciples see the invisible hand of God moving in, through, and beyond mere current events. The question frees them and us from being trapped in the sorrowful recounting of current events. It frees them and us to look to God's greater plan and purpose.

Providence teaches us that history is not a blind, aimless march into nothingness and meaninglessness. History is the recorded orchestration of God's work in redeeming mankind through the cross and resurrection of our Lord. There really *is* a Man behind the curtain. *Do* pay attention to Him! He is God, and He wants us to observe His providence and plan. Looking to His providence reminds us that current events and history are going somewhere. God is up to something good! The greatest proof of that is Jesus is alive—not dead.

Redirects Us from the Law to the Gospel

It is interesting that each of the gospel writers tells us about these good Jewish followers of Jesus obeying the law, specifically the Sabbath commands. Some people will make much of this detail, but they will not make what they should of it.

Notice how the angels' question redirects them. The question turns them away from the law to the gospel—to the good news of Jesus' crucifixion, burial, and resurrection. The death, burial, and resurrection free us from having to keep the law in order to be reconciled with and justified before God. Christ has fulfilled the law in our place. So now we turn to God through faith in Christ.

Jesus teaches this about Himself in Matthew 5:17: "Do not think that I came to destroy the Law or the Prophets. I did not come to destroy but to fulfill." Paul teaches the same truth in Romans 1:17: "For in [the gospel] the righteousness of God is revealed from faith to faith; as it is written, 'The just shall live by faith.'" In many ways, the remainder of the book simply expands and explains the truth of Romans 1:17. For example, Romans 10:4 proclaims, "For Christ is the end of the law for righteousness to everyone who believes." Romans 4:25 explicitly connects righteousness and the resurrection: "Who was delivered up because of our offenses, and was raised because of our justification."

The resurrection turns us from law-keeping to gospel-believing and from self-righteousness to an alien righteousness in Jesus Christ. It turns us from trying to earn God's love by our good deeds to freely accepting God's love as a gift through faith in His Son. The resurrection turns us from the death the law requires to the eternal life that Jesus purchased.

Christian, our every moment can be a turning again, a reorienting and redirection to the gospel of our Lord. It is our privilege to keep preaching the gospel to ourselves and to one another rather than listening to the condemnation of the law. Every day we get to look deeper and deeper into the good news of Jesus' death and resurrection so that we may live in the riches of God's grace through Christ. "Why do you seek the living among the dead?" reminds us that we live in the completed work of Jesus Christ—sins completely forgiven, atonement completely made, justification completely declared, adoption completely accomplished, and glory completely secured. It is finished!

The women came to the tomb thinking about what the law required and forbade. But with that question—"Why do you seek the living among the dead?"—they discovered that though they came like good Jews, they could leave forgiven, justified saints. They could live in the resurrection realities of the gospel through faith.

Every living person can live in the reality of the resurrection too. The gospel is for everyone. God's law requires the sinner's death as the penalty for sin. Death is an agonizing judgment, a curse from God, an enemy that separates those who die in sin from God forever. But the good news is that Jesus Christ lived the perfectly obedient life that you and I could not. That is how He became our righteousness. Then Jesus Christ died and suffered God's wrath and judgment in our place on the cross. That is how He takes away our sin and guilt. Three days later God raised Jesus from death to life to prove He had accepted Jesus' sacrifice on our behalf. Now, God the Father calls all sinners to repent of their sin and to trust in Jesus Christ alone as their God and Savior. Everyone who truly repents and believes will be rescued from death, forgiven of sin, made alive again through faith, and live eternally with God forever. That is the wonderfully good news. All those who trust in Jesus—even if they die—will live again in the power of the resurrection and in the eternal fellowship of God's love.

Do you want to live in God's acceptance and love? Then turn *from* sin and *to* Jesus as your God and Master, who saves sinners from God's wrath through the cross and resurrection.

Redirects Us from Grief to Joy

This final point should be obvious. If Jesus is alive and not dead, then all who trust in Him have the supreme reason to rejoice. I think the apostle Peter, an eyewitness to the life, death, and resurrection of the Lord, expressed this best in 1 Peter 1. He shows us the connection between life, the Lord's resurrection, our new birth, and our joy. Peter was one of those mourning disciples taken from grief to joy.

See how Peter opens his letter with joyful praise: "Blessed be the God and Father of our Lord Jesus Christ" (v. 3). Peter begins this way because he sees the connection between our new birth and the Lord's resurrection: "who according to His abundant mercy has *begotten us again* to a living hope *through the resurrection of Jesus Christ from the dead*" (emphasis added).

This joining of the new birth and the resurrection is the source of our great grief-conquering joy. Peter explains, "In this you greatly rejoice, though now for a little while, if need be, you have been grieved by various trials" (v. 6). Because of the resurrection, we have a new birth and an eternal inheritance that gives us joy and praise greater than our grief. So much so, Peter writes, "whom having not seen you love. Though now you do not see Him, yet believing, you rejoice with joy inexpressible and full of glory, receiving the end of your faith—the salvation of your souls" (vv. 8–9). "Joy inexpressible and full of glory" awaits all those who confront their grief and trials with the reality of the resurrection and eternal inheritance we have through Christ.

Would you be happy and full of joy in this life and the life to come? Embrace and remember the resurrection. Because Jesus was raised from the dead and keeps our inheritance in heaven by His power, He puts our joy safely beyond the reach of all our enemies, including death. If you would know pure joy, trust that Jesus has done it all.

Would you be happy now and forever? Put your hope in a revolution greater than anything Copernicus and science could ever imagine. Put your hope in the revolution Jesus accomplished through the resurrection, and you will be reoriented from death to life, from the cross to the resurrection, from emotion to God's Word, from current events to God's providence, from the law to the gospel, and from grief to joy.

For Further Gazing and Reflection

1. Read Luke 24:1–12. Who asks, "Why do you seek the living among the dead"? Who is seeking the living among the dead—and why?

2. Often in the Bible, dawn, or early morning, is the time God uses to make new revelations. Sunrise is when the Lord surprises His people. What were the surprises the Lord had for the seekers on the Sunday morning described in this chapter?

3. Abraham, Jesus, and the apostle Paul provide examples of people living in light of the resurrection. How have other people in the Bible shown that they live in light of the resurrection? How do you show that you live in light of the resurrection?

4. Why is it important for us to redirect our emotions in difficult situations to Scripture? What effect will that have on our thinking?

5. What does the angels' question teach us about God's sovereign providence?

6. What is the connection between the Lord's resurrection and our joy? (See 1 Peter 1:3–9.)

Chapter 5

Do You Not Know These Things?

Cleopas said, "Are You the only stranger in Jeru-salem, and have You not known the things which happened there in these days?"

—LUKE 24:18

Epistemology is a fancy word for any theory of how we know things. How do you know that you know something? That is epistemology. Few people walk around using the word *epistemology* or debating various theories for how human beings know things. The next time you attend a dinner party, you can amaze your friends by referring to "the interesting epistemological foundation for that claim." They will either think you are really smart or that you are really a show-off. So use it carefully.

Even though we rarely use the word *epistemology* in everyday conversation, we all have some theory for how we know what we know. We might say things such as, "I just know it's true." In other words, we are relying on a subjective feeling or an inward assurance to determine what we know. Or, when we say, "The facts speak for themselves," or, "It's a proven scientific fact," we place our confidence in observable facts to help us know things. Such statements rely on the processes of testing and retesting various phenomena to build a knowledge base. Or, someone might say, "Let's be reasonable." In such cases, the rules of logic take center stage in our epistemology. Finally, someone might say, "I know because someone told me." That is an epistemological claim too. We come to know things by someone else's testimony.

All these everyday expressions represent different ways of knowing. However, each of these approaches to knowledge has strengths and weaknesses. Science does not get everything right. Reason may break down. Testimonies can be unreliable. Facts have to be interpreted. And what we think is true and right based on our feelings can just as easily be the burrito we ate last night. We have to use all these epistemological tools, but we need more. If we are to know that we know that we know, then we need a more reliable way of knowing than anything that originates with us.

When it comes to the most important matters in life, we do not want to be left not knowing what is true and real. Does she love me? Is there a cure? Am I right to feel the way I feel about life? Is there a God? How do we know the resurrection happened? How do I know my sins will be forgiven and I will go to heaven when I die? The big questions require sound epistemology, a way of knowing that surpasses our limited abilities.

We have come to our final meditation on the cross and resurrection. In the preceding chapters, we have been captivated by the meaning of Jesus' crucifixion and resurrection. We have attempted to explain what happened in those three days and why it matters for us. In this chapter, with God's help, we want to make the cross and resurrection of Jesus quite personal. We want to ask ourselves, "How does it matter for me individually and personally?" To do that, we want to consider our epistemology: How do we know these things to be true? Is there a way of knowing more reliable than testimony, feeling, perception, facts, or science?

Three Insufficient Ways of Knowing the Truth about Jesus and the Resurrection

Luke 24:13 tells us the disciples were traveling on "that same day." What day is that? It was the "first day of the week," or Sunday. It was the day the women went to the tomb "early in the morning" only to discover "the stone rolled away" and the body of the Lord Jesus missing (v. 1). It was the day the women "told all these things to the eleven and to all the rest" (v. 9). It was a day of great mourning because three days earlier Jesus was crucified and buried. And it was a day of great confusion because they did not know what happened to the body.

On that day, these two disciples walked to "a village called Emmaus." Verse 13 tells us Emmaus was seven miles from Jerusalem. It was a long walk. To pass the time and to make sense of things, the two disciples "talked together of all these things which had happened" (v. 14). They probably talked the way many people talk: not too deeply about their feelings, rehearsing the facts, pausing to consider solutions, wanting to regain control.

Three things happen with these two disciples in this text. First, "Jesus Himself drew near and went with them"

(v. 15). They experience a post-resurrection appearance of the Lord. With all their senses—sight, hearing, perhaps touch and smell, and later taste—they encounter Jesus. Second, they explain to Jesus the facts of the last several days (vv. 18–24). They explain who Jesus was, as they understood Him, and what Jesus did, including His death and the eyewitness testimony of the empty tomb. Third, Jesus explains the Scriptures concerning Himself and stops to eat with them (vv. 25–32). Each of these experiences illustrates three insufficient ways of knowing the truth about who Jesus is.

Physical Senses Alone Are Insufficient
Jesus walks with them, talks with them, and cooks and eats with them. Perhaps Jesus laid His hand on their shoulders, or they shook hands when they first met on the road to Emmaus. We marvel at what it must have been like to have a multisensory encounter with the resurrected Lord. But the truly marvelous thing is "their eyes were restrained, so that they did not know Him" (v. 16). They were physically with Jesus, but they had no idea who Jesus was. Their physical senses failed them. Physical data alone was insufficient for grasping the truth about the Son of God.

We like to think that if Jesus showed up today, we would recognize Him right away. Such a belief reveals our pride, does it not? Recognizing Jesus is not a matter of physical sight or sensory perception. It is remarkable that when Jesus appeared to any of the disciples for the first time, they did not immediately recognize Him. Mary Magdalene did not recognize the Lord on sight:

But Mary stood outside by the tomb weeping, and as she wept she stooped down and looked into the tomb. And she saw two angels in white sitting, one at the head and the other at the feet, where the body of Jesus had lain. Then they said to her, "Woman, why are you weeping?"

She said to them, "Because they have taken away my Lord, and I do not know where they have laid Him."

Now when she had said this, she turned around and saw Jesus standing there, and did not know that it was Jesus. Jesus said to her, "Woman, why are you weeping? Whom are you seeking?"

She, supposing Him to be the gardener, said to Him, "Sir, if You have carried Him away, tell me where You have laid Him, and I will take Him away."

Jesus said to her, "Mary!"

She turned and said to Him, "Rabboni!" (which is to say, Teacher). (John 20:11–16)

The male disciples were not any quicker to recognize Jesus. Consider that famous passage in John 21:1–7, when Jesus appeared to the disciples while they were fishing:

After these things Jesus showed Himself again to the disciples at the Sea of Tiberias, and in this way He showed Himself: Simon Peter, Thomas called the Twin, Nathanael of Cana in Galilee, the sons of Zebedee, and two others of His disciples were together. Simon Peter said to them, "I am going fishing."

They said to him, "We are going with you also." They went out and immediately got into the boat, and that night they caught nothing. But when the morning had now come, Jesus stood on the shore; yet the disciples did not know that it was Jesus. Then Jesus said to them, "Children, have you any food?"

They answered Him, "No."

And He said to them, "Cast the net on the right side of the boat, and you will find some." So they cast, and now they were not able to draw it in because of the multitude of fish.

Therefore that disciple whom Jesus loved said to Peter, "It is the Lord!" Now when Simon Peter heard that it was the Lord, he put on his outer garment (for he had removed it), and plunged into the sea.

Mary, Peter, the disciples, and the two on the road to Emmaus saw, spoke with, and heard Jesus. But our physical senses are insufficient for knowing and recognizing Jesus for who He truly is.

Facts Alone Are Insufficient—Even If They Are Firsthand Eyewitness Testimonies

In verses 17–24, Jesus asks the two disciples what they are discussing. The question froze them in their tracks and changed their expression: "They stood still, their faces downcast" (v. 17). They reply in verse 18, "Are You the only stranger in Jerusalem, and have You not known the things which happened there in these days?" We might translate that, "Where have *You* been? You must not be from around here. Don't You know what's happening? Haven't You heard what's going on?" The irony is obvious, is it not? Jesus did not need to hear about these things. He endured them.

But what grabs our attention is the report they give in verses 19–24. The two disciples run down the facts about Jesus and recent events. They mention that Jesus was a powerful prophet in both word and deed. They tell of how the religious leaders sentenced Jesus to death and how He was crucified. They even mention their own hopeful feelings, believing Jesus was the one to redeem Israel. Then they give the facts about His burial three days ago and the amazing eyewitness testimony from the women and from the male disciples: the body was no longer in the tomb. They have the facts down cold. They had witnessed much of this, and what they had not witnessed themselves they heard from other eyewitnesses.

And yet they do not recognize Jesus when they speak with Him face-to-face. It is not enough to know the facts about Jesus' life. There are many people who know the facts of Jesus' life but do not recognize who He truly is. Churches are filled with people who say they believe in God—but who would not recognize Jesus if He sat next to them!

James 2:19 reminds us that our belief and knowledge of Jesus may barely surpass that of demons. "You believe that there is one God. You do well. Even the demons believe—and tremble!" Merely saying, "I believe in God" or knowing some facts about Jesus will not save a person from the wrath of God to come. Such knowledge or faith may even be *worse* than a demon's. For demons, James tells us, have sense enough to shudder in fear when they say there is a God. They say it with *trembling*. But sinners say, "I believe in God" and never shiver once while they engage in immoral sex, drink themselves into a stupor, lie, curse, steal, cheat, grumble, and so on.

The two disciples on the road to Emmaus believe all the facts about Jesus, but they still miss something. They are religiously devout, but they do not recognize the very Founder of their religion. Facts alone will not get us there.

Bible Study Alone Is Insufficient

How would you like to have Jesus lead your Bible study? In verses 25–27, that is exactly what happens with these two disciples. They give their report, and then Jesus does two things. He rebukes them, and He teaches them the Bible. They asked Jesus, "Do you not know the things that happened here?" In return, Jesus asks them the same question in verses 25–26: "O foolish ones, and slow of heart to believe in all that the prophets have spoken! Ought not the Christ to have suffered these things and to enter into His glory?" In other words, "What's wrong with *you?* Do you not know that this was written of the Messiah? Do you not know these things?"

Then the Lord leads them in a Bible study through the entire Old Testament: "Beginning at Moses and all the Prophets, He expounded to them in all the Scriptures the things concerning Himself" (v. 27). Jesus explains the recent events in light of the Bible's truth. But even with Jesus as their Bible teacher, they still did not recognize Him. Bible knowledge alone is insufficient for recognizing Jesus as He really is.

There are many people who will tell you, "I read my Bible every day," and yet they do not seem to us as those who really know Jesus. There are people who have heard the Bible preached and sang the truth of the Bible in church for twenty or thirty years, and yet they do not seem to have come to a true knowledge of Jesus. Sitting in a church for twenty years does not make you a Christian any more than putting rocks in an oven makes them biscuits.

Truly recognizing Jesus is not a matter of having a lot of Bible facts. Illiterate people who cannot read the Bible may know Jesus deeply, while New Testament scholars teaching in leading universities could not identify Jesus in a police line-up if He were the only one with a crown of thorns who was bleeding from His wrists and side. We are not closer to Jesus because we know more of the Bible than others. It may be that such knowledge only "puffs up" (1 Cor. 8:1).

Experiences will not bring us saving knowledge of Christ. The bare facts will not get us there. Bible knowledge and religious activity will not save us. These three things are insufficient for knowing Jesus as He truly is. We need something more reliable.

One Infallible Way of Knowing the Truth about Jesus and the Resurrection

Only one infallible way of knowing the truth about who Jesus really is and the power of His resurrection exists. We must have our eyes opened by God.

Verse 16 says, "Their eyes were restrained, so that they did not know Him," or, as the *New International Version* puts it, "They were kept from recognizing him." Who kept them from recognizing Jesus? God the Father did. They would not recognize Jesus until "their eyes were opened and they knew Him" (v. 31). Knowing Jesus requires that God supernaturally open our eyes with spiritual sight. Such revelation is the one infallible way of knowing the truth about Jesus.

In fact, we are *unable* to know the truth about Jesus in a saving way unless God reveals the Son to us. Matthew records Jesus praying,

> At that time Jesus answered and said, "I thank You, Father, Lord of heaven and earth, that *You have hidden these things from* the wise and prudent and have revealed them to babes. Even so, Father, for so it seemed good in Your sight. All things have been delivered to Me by My Father, and no one knows the Son except the Father. Nor does anyone know the Father except the Son, *and the one* to whom the Son wills to reveal *Him.* (11:25–27, emphasis added)

The Father must reveal the truth about Jesus, and Jesus must reveal the Father. The Father gives the truth about Jesus to some but not others. Knowledge of Jesus belongs to His disciples, which baffled even the disciples: "The disciples came and said to Him, 'Why do You speak to them in parables?' He answered and said to them, '*Because it has been given to you to know the mysteries of the kingdom of heaven, but to them it has not been given*'" (Matt. 13:10–11).

Man confidently hopes in his own wisdom and knowledge. We think science will prove everything. We believe our interpretation of the facts leads us to truth. We even believe our unstable feelings are reliable guides to knowledge. But we do not know as we ought to know unless the all-knowing One teaches us. As Paul plainly puts it, "The natural man does not receive the things of the Spirit of God, for they are foolishness to him: nor can he know them, because they are spiritually discerned" (1 Cor. 2:14).

Divine revelation provides the one infallible epistemology. Yet divine revelation is that one source of knowledge that sinners work hard to ignore and reject. If you reject God's revelation, you reject the only perfect way of knowing things as they really are. You reject the only coherent and unified source of truth there is. And that's why life goes crazy. How can our lives not go out of control if we reject the truth of God and the God of truth?

In order to recognize and accept Jesus for who He is, we must be born again. The Spirit of God must give us a new heart and new eyes of faith so that we can understand the things of God and the secrets of the kingdom of heaven. The Father must open our eyes so we can see Jesus. Until God opens our eyes to who He really is in Christ, we remain blind to ultimate truth.

Has God opened your eyes yet? Do you see with the sight that He alone can give? How would you know that you see and recognize Jesus for who He is?

Three Important Insights We Must Embrace

If God has opened our eyes, then there are three things we must embrace in order to know Jesus as He truly is.

Jesus Has Come in the Flesh

The early disciples who lived with Jesus would have known that He came in the flesh. It seems like an obvious thing to say. But early in Christian history, some people began to doubt and deny Jesus' incarnation. Such denials are an old problem dating back to the days of the apostles. These problems continue with us today in liberal and New Age ideas.

People may deny the bodily reality of Christ in a couple ways. Some deny the incarnation itself. They prefer to talk about "the Christ Spirit" rather than the real Jesus. They distinguish between the so-called "Christ of Easter" and the "Jesus of history." They make a false distinction and thereby deny the reality of Christ's bodily existence.

Others do not deny that Jesus lived a real bodily life; they deny instead the bodily resurrection. They maintain that Christ was raised *spiritually* and sometimes head off in New Age directions. But notice in Luke 24:3 that "they went in and did not find *the body* of the Lord Jesus." Why the emphasis on "the body"? In biblical Christianity, the body of our Lord is critical to His saving purpose. Hebrews 2:14–17 teaches us that because Jesus took on our physical bodies and our human nature, He can be our High Priest who sacrifices Himself for us. Romans 4:25 tells us that Jesus was put to death (a real bodily death) for our sins and raised (a real bodily resurrection) for our justification.

To deny the real flesh of Christ—in His incarnation or resurrection—is to deny the possibility of salvation through Christ. If there is no crucifixion, then there is no atonement for sin. If there is no resurrection from the dead, then there is no victory over death, no eternal life, and no justification with God. If Christ has not come in the flesh, then there is no gospel at all!

The apostles teach us not to believe anyone who denies that Jesus came in the flesh. "By this you know the Spirit of God: Every spirit that confesses that Jesus Christ has come in the flesh is of God, and every spirit that does not confess that Jesus Christ has come in the flesh is not of God. And this is the spirit of the Antichrist, which you have heard was coming, and is now already in the world" (1 John 4:2–3). Whether we acknowledge or deny that Jesus came in the flesh is as serious and important as whether we know Jesus or whether we follow the spirit of the Antichrist.

Are your eyes opened by God to see and believe that Jesus came in the flesh?

Jesus Is God's Unique Son

The disciples had not fully grasped this yet. They heard it said several times but still had not truly embraced it yet. They did not know that Jesus is God's unique Son despite Peter's famous profession in Matthew 16:13–17:

> When Jesus came into the region of Caesarea Philippi, He asked His disciples, saying, "Who do men say that I, the Son of Man, am?"
>
> So they said, "Some say John the Baptist, some Elijah, and others Jeremiah or one of the prophets."
>
> He said to them, "But who do you say that I am?"

> *Simon Peter answered and said, "You are the Christ, the Son of the living God."*
>
> *Jesus answered and said to him, "Blessed are you, Simon Bar-Jonah, for flesh and blood has not revealed this to you, but My Father who is in heaven."* (emphasis added)

They did not know that Jesus is God's unique Son despite the Father's own testimony at the transfiguration in Matthew 17:1–5:

> Now after six days Jesus took Peter, James, and John his brother, led them up on a high mountain by themselves; and He was transfigured before them. His face shone like the sun, and His clothes became as white as the light. And behold, Moses and Elijah appeared to them, talking with Him. Then Peter answered and said to Jesus, "Lord, it is good for us to be here; if You wish, let us make here three tabernacles: one for You, one for Moses, and one for Elijah."
>
> While he was still speaking, behold, a bright cloud overshadowed them; and suddenly a voice came out of the cloud, saying, *"This is My beloved Son, in whom I am well pleased. Hear Him!"* (emphasis added)

They did not grasp that Jesus is God's unique Son despite the testimony of the Gentile centurion at Jesus' crucifixion: "So when the centurion and those with him, who were guarding Jesus, saw the earthquake and the things that had happened, they feared greatly, saying, 'Truly this was the Son of God'" (Matt. 27:54).

Despite three separate testimonies, the disciples continued to miss this truth. As Jesus said to Peter, "Flesh and blood cannot reveal this, only the Father in heaven." There needed to be a more complete revelation, a more complete opening of the eyes. This is why the resurrection was so vital. The resurrection of the Lord Jesus was designed to declare conclusively that Jesus is the unique Son of God. Paul writes "concerning His Son Jesus Christ our Lord, who was born of the *seed of David according to the flesh,* and *declared to be the Son of God with power* according to the spirit of holiness, *by the resurrection from the dead*" (Romans 1:3–4, emphasis added).

To celebrate Easter truly, to celebrate the resurrection of the Lord, is to see in it the Holy Spirit's powerful declaration that Jesus is the Son of God. It is to sing what the centurion exclaimed in fear, "Surely He was the Son of God!" We can have no proper celebration of Easter unless our eyes are opened to the fact that Jesus is the unique Son of God and we embrace it with the eyes of faith.

Do you know these things? Are your eyes opened by God to see and believe?

We Know That Jesus Is Lord
That Jesus came in the flesh and He is God's unique Son are not abstract, distant theological facts. Do not let your mind get foggy thinking about theology here. All of this comes home personally in a third thing we must have our eyes opened to see: Jesus is Lord.

Unless we recognize Him as the ruler of all creation and of our individual lives, then we do not recognize Him as He truly is. We are not saved from God's judgment. We are not yet born again. We are like these two disciples on the road to Emmaus—religious but not recognizing the truth for ourselves.

God must open our eyes to see this third important fact too. First Corinthians 12:3 tells us that "no one can say that Jesus is Lord except by the Holy Spirit." This does not mean people cannot make their physical voices say, "Jesus is Lord." You can train a parrot to physically say such things. This means that when it comes to really grasping Jesus' lordship—to accept Him as our personal ruler and king and to obey Him as our God—we cannot do these things without the supernatural work of the Holy Spirit giving us the ability to do so.

A couple decades ago, "the lordship salvation" controversy broke out among evangelical Christians. On one side were people who said Jesus can be a person's Savior yet not his Lord. Such people could genuinely trust in Christ but not have Christ ruling their lives. On the other side were people who said there is no way to receive Jesus as Savior without also receiving Him as Lord. They argued that to receive Jesus at all, we have to receive Him as He offers Himself in the gospel—and in the gospel Jesus offers Himself as one Savior and Lord of all. The two things cannot be separated. The second group is correct. Jesus *is* Lord. Christ's lordship is one of the earliest Christian professions of faith, asserted in 1 Corinthians, one of the earliest New Testament letters.

Jesus Himself tells us what it means to call Him "Lord." It means to obey His rule and authority in our lives. Jesus told His disciples in Luke 6 a parable of two men who each built a house. One built his house on sand, and when the rains and floods came, that house came crashing down. The other built his house on rock, and when the rains and floods came, that house stood strong. Do you remember how Jesus introduced that parable? He asked in Luke 6:46: "Why do you call Me 'Lord, Lord,' and not do the things which I say?" In other words, "How can I be your Lord if you do not obey Me?" The entire parable teaches us to submit to Jesus' lordship in obedience to His Word. The man who builds on the rock recognizes that Jesus is Lord and, in recognition of that, obeys what Jesus teaches. The man who builds his house on the rock comes to Jesus and puts His words into practice. That man survived. The man who had no foundation in obedience to God's Word was completely destroyed.

Conclusion

Do you know these things? Do you know Jesus? On what are you basing your knowledge of Christ: your emotions, experiences, knowledge of the facts, or religious activity such as Bible study? Or do you know Jesus because God has opened your eyes to realize He has come in the flesh to offer Himself as a sacrifice for sin and to be raised from the grave? Do you know Jesus because God has opened your eyes to recognize through the resurrection that Jesus is the only begotten and unique Son of God? Do you know Jesus because God has opened your eyes to see and obey Him as your own Lord and Savior?

Or do you *not* know these things? Have your eyes *not* been opened? Unless your eyes are open and you are given faith, you will die in your sins, and after that will be God's eternal wrath and judgment.

If your eyes have *not* been opened, then open your mouth. Pray to the Lord for the gift of sight, so that seeing with the eyes of faith, you may believe in Jesus and be saved. Call on God to give you the gift of faith so that you may live forever in His love and joy and share in the wonder of His glory and resurrection.

For Further Gazing and Reflection

1. Read Luke 24:13–35. Cleopas asks the "stranger," "Do you not know these things?" What "things" does he mean?

2. What is *epistemology*?

3. Explain why physical senses alone are not sufficient for knowing the truth about Jesus. Give an example from Scripture that demonstrates this truth.

4. Why are facts and Bible study insufficient for knowing the truth about Jesus?

5. What is the one infallible way of knowing the truth about Jesus and the resurrection? Consider whether this is the basis for your epistemology.

6. Why is it important for us to understand that Jesus came in the flesh?

7. Despite the testimonies of Simon Peter, God the Father at Jesus' transfiguration, and the centurion at the cross, the disciples still did not grasp that Jesus is God's unique Son. What had to happen so that they could understand this truth?

8. Explain why you agree or disagree with this statement: Jesus can be a person's Savior yet not his Lord.

9. What have you come to see more clearly as you have stared at Jesus through the lens of the five questions in this book?

*Other resources
from*
**REFORMATION
HERITAGE BOOKS**

"May We Meet in the Heavenly World":
The Piety of Lemuel Haynes

Thabiti M. Anyabwile

978-1-60178-065-2   Paperback, 152 pages

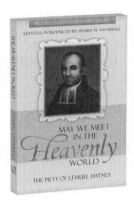

In *"May We Meet in the Heavenly World"*, Thabiti M. Anyabwile introduces us to the New England preacher, Lemuel Haynes (1753–1833). Through both the biographical essay and the selections from Haynes's writings, readers are sure to perceive an Edwardsian sense of spirituality that ever lived in view of eternity. Well acquainted with difficulties, suffering, and death, Haynes's ministry was infused with the unfailing hope of heaven.

"This well-chosen selection from Lemuel Haynes's writings represents a significant part of the earliest African-American engagements with the Reformed theological tradition. In that tradition Haynes and his black contemporaries, both American and British, found a language of justice and inspiration that allowed them to criticize slavery and racial prejudice, and to offer a Christian vision of a free society. *"May We Meet in the Heavenly World"* can be recommended to students of Christian theology and of American history."

— JOHN SAILLANT, author of *Black Puritan, Black Republican: The Life and Thought of Lemuel Haynes, 1753–1833*

Memoirs of the Way Home:
Ezra and Nehemiah as a Call to Conversion

Gerald M. Bilkes

978-1-60178-264-9   Paperback, 200 pages

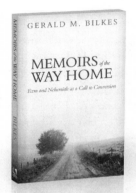

Author Gerald Bilkes explains that in the books of Ezra and Nehemiah, we have two first-person accounts, or memoirs, of Israel's return from exile to the Promised Land. In this winsome Bible study, with questions for individual or group reflection at the end of each chapter, the author introduces readers to the lesser-known Old Testament books of Ezra and Nehemiah and helps us understand that these are not the records of historic feats but rather the confessions of a humble prodigal on a profoundly spiritual journey home. With pastoral warmth, Bilkes demonstrates these biblical memoirs' relevance for us today as they challenge us to consider whether we are in the far country or, by grace, on our way back home to God.

"Few people know the history of Ezra and Nehemiah and their God-given work to reestablish Israel in the Promised Land after their Babylonian exile. *Memoirs of the Way Home* offers an easily accessible survey and devotional reflection upon these overlooked but nevertheless vibrant books of the Bible. Readers will certainly benefit from this simple exploration of the many rich and vital truths that we find in Ezra and Nehemiah and the way Gerald Bilkes connects them to Christ and the church."

— J. V. FESKO, academic dean and professor of systematic and historical theology, Westminster Seminary California

Life in Christ:
Becoming and Being a
Disciple of the Lord Jesus Christ

Jeremy Walker

978-1-60178-274-8   Paperback, 152 pages

"To be a disciple of Jesus Christ is to be in a position of privilege and blessing beyond anything the world might offer," begins author Jeremy Walker. *Life in Christ* explores the unsearchable riches of the Christian pilgrimage and traces its trajectory, highlighting key elements in the believer's experience. Do you wrestle with assurance? Have you grasped the engagement demanded in Christian living? Do you find the way wearying at times? Do you struggle with your Christian identity? Walker provides instruction for Christians to assess their own standing and progress in the faith—exhorting and equipping and always pointing them ahead to the hope of Christ's glory. Along the way, he encourages God's people to live a life to the praise of His glory as he examines some basic truths that establish and direct a true child of God.

"In this well-ordered book, Jeremy Walker provides a straightforward presentation of what it is to become and live as a disciple of Jesus Christ. Following Christ is not a matter of secondary importance but should be of critical concern for every reader of this book. Each page is saturated with scriptural truths that are easy to read but challenging to apply regarding this vital subject of discipleship. I highly recommend this work, which is doctrinally sound, persuasively presented, and pastorally related."

—STEVEN J. LAWSON, senior pastor, Christ Fellowship
Baptist Church, Mobile, Alabama

A Labor of Love:
Puritan Pastoral Priorities

J. Stephen Yuille
Foreword by Steve Lawson

978–1–60178–266–3   Paperback, 152 pages

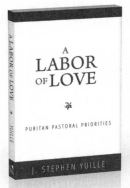

Driven by the desire to be successful, pastors are tempted to judge their ministries by the worldly standards of power, prestige, privilege, and prosperity. In contrast, J. Stephen Yuille reorients our understanding of pastoral ministry by presenting a standard of excellence measured by faithfulness, humility, and submission to God—even when the results look unsuccessful in the eyes of the world. Drawing from the Puritan minister George Swinnock, Yuille expands on a list of sixteen heartfelt desires that Swinnock expressed for his own pastoral ministry. Yuille's reflections on these timeless priorities are full of biblical insights and pastoral wisdom. The book ends with Swinnock's farewell sermon to his congregation, which serves as an encouraging example for all pastors who desire to love their people in Christ. This book is a valuable guide for pastors as they seek to labor and love in the service of Christ.

> "This book is an accessible and challenging introduction to the pastoral office and its duties as understood by the Puritans. In an age when the notion of office is either downplayed or understood in a confused manner, the Puritans still have the power to speak with force and clarity. Dr. Yuille has done us a great service in producing such a work."

> —CARL R. TRUEMAN, Paul Woolley Professor of Church History,
> Westminster Theological Seminary, Philadelphia